A GIRL GROWS UP

FOURTH EDITION

BY RUTH FEDDER

Northern Arizona University, Flagstaff, Arizona

McGRAW-HILL BOOK COMPANY
NEW YORK · TORONTO · LONDON · SYDNEY

A Girl Grows Up

Library of Congress Catalog Card Number: AC 67-10514

To You—From the Author

EARLIER EDITIONS of *A Girl Grows Up* were enthusiastically received because girls said the book helped them to work out answers to many of their burning questions. Apparently teen-agers do not want ready-made solutions to problems they face daily: they want a sense of direction as they seek answers to questions which recur, with ever-mounting insistence, to them all: Who am I? How can I understand myself? What does growing up mean? What can I do? Where am I going? How do I make friends? How can I understand my parents better? What does it mean to be a woman? How can I prepare to be a good wife and mother? How can I find my place vocationally? The fourth edition of this book discusses basic questions like these with today's teen-agers.

Are today's teen-agers so different from those of a decade ago when the preceding edition of this book was published? They are more numerous, wealthier, and more sophisticated. Their number grew from 15 million in 1955 to 25 million in 1965; in other words, a million teen-agers a year have been added to our population. In 1967, over one-half of the population of the United States will be under twenty-five!

Today's teen-agers are wealthier than they were ten years ago. Today, they average $13 a week in spending money as against $9 ten years ago. Moreover, they *earn* much of this money. Whereas 22 per cent of the girls had part-time jobs in 1955, 30 per cent were working in 1965; 35 per cent of the boys worked ten years ago, while 40 per cent were employed in 1965.

Clearly, teen-age years are critical ones. Teen-agers want and need reliable information about fundamentals of behavior.

They must resolve many questions, questions like those in the first paragraph. These are not new questions, but they are questions which each generation must answer in its own way if its members are to be happy, well-adjusted human beings. Today's teen-agers describe the search for answers as the "search for identity." Essentially, the search is for self-realization, and it calls for sensitive understanding and wise interpretation of all you can learn from every field of knowledge. A philosopher centuries ago summed it up in the phrase "Know thyself."

Teen-age girls from various backgrounds contributed their ideas to this book: there were girls with many cultural and economic advantages and girls with comparatively few; and there were girls from many states who lived in communities that ranged from mountain to desert, from suburban areas and rural villages to industrial cities. These girls had many different religious, national, and racial backgrounds. They were sophomores, juniors, and seniors, and they represented all degrees of academic achievement.

The material in this book has been arranged to help girls think through their own problems. After a short introduction (Chapter 1), questions about personality development and emotional maturity are considered (Chapters 2, 3, 4, and 5). Against this background, problems of family relationships are specifically discussed (Chapter 6). There follows consideration of boy-and-girl relationships (Chapter 7), vocational adjustment (Chapter 8), the use of leisure time (Chapter 9), and the development of a philosophy of life (Chapter 10).

Today's fashions—in clothing, hairstyles, and cosmetics—make teen-agers appear to be more youthfully sophisticated than they used to be. In addition, teen-agers actually are assuming growing responsibilities at home and at school. Aside from the jobs they hold, 65 per cent of the girls baby-sit at home (as do 20 per cent of the boys), 75 per cent of them are responsible for the family shopping, and 65 per cent are responsible for the housecleaning. In 1965, 20 per cent of the boys helped with housecleaning.

More teen-agers are now finishing high school, and more are going to college—55 per cent of today's high school graduates as compared to 40 per cent in 1955. Within the high school and college curricula, courses are more advanced and more sophisticated. Even the hobbies girls cultivate indicate a concern for their future: 16 per cent of all girls in 1965 stated that cooking was their favorite hobby, as against 8 per cent in 1955!

Society's growing demands on teen-agers for maturity at home and in school may be responsible for their yearning for close personal relationships. Ten years ago, 1 fourteen-year-old girl out of 200 was "going steady." Today, 1 out of 9 reports that she is going steady, although she may mean by this only that she has had three successive dates with one boy. Nevertheless, dating and going steady earlier are leading some teen-agers into emotional involvements which they find they are ill-equipped to handle or into early marriages for which they are not ready. Such girls say that they don't want to take chances on not having a date for a weekend, so they arrange to have a steady companion. The peak marrying year for girls is now eighteen.

Interpretation of this material is based on the best psychological knowledge available, with concentration on the commonest difficulties girls seem to meet in the process of growing up. These difficulties are examined, and the behavior of some girls in response to various situations and conditions is described. Examples of mature and immature behavior are given; thus girls may see where they stand and begin to interpret their behavior.

During the years since the previous edition of *A Girl Grows Up*, the author has moved from the eastern to the western part of the country. She has talked with boys and girls in cities, towns, suburbs, and rural areas. After these discussions, she wrote down ideas about questions which had concerned these young people. Many girls and boys, individually and in groups, have read carefully all the material contained in this edition.

This edition presents some new material in each chapter and new illustrations. It also contains a new, up-to-date bibliography for girls who want to read further in areas of special interest. It is the author's hope that teen-age girls may find this edition as helpful to them as it apparently has been to girls whom the author has known personally.

The author wishes to thank the boys and girls as well as the professional associates who made this book possible. The following persons gave helpful advice and encouragement during its initial preparation: Professor Esther Lloyd-Jones and the late Professor Sarah Sturtevant, both of Teachers College, Columbia University; Alice V. Keliher, former distinguished professor, State College, Jersey City, New Jersey; Dr. Bruce Robinson, former director, Department of Child Guidance, Board of Education, Newark, New Jersey. In assembling the bibliography, the help of Margaret Scoggin, Coordinator, Young People's Services, New York City Public Library, was invaluable. The author of the poem at the end of the last chapter, unfortunately, is unknown.

Sedona, Arizona   **Ruth Fedder**

Contents

Contents

CHAPTER ONE

Growing Up

EVERYONE THOUGHT that Patti and Alice were the best of friends. And, in a way, they were. Tall, pretty, black-haired Alice was almost always with small, slender Patti with the sophisticated blonde hair-do. Both were bright girls. Both did well in school. Alice's name consistently was found among the top two or three on the Honors list, but Patti was usually on the list too—although she would occasionally make a low grade, especially when there was snow. Patti said she supposed she'd been "born on skis" for "when the white stuff falls, I can't contain myself—I've got to ski. I forget all my troubles when I'm skiing."

Troubles? Does a girl like Patti have troubles? "Everything kind of came to a head at midterm—imagine, in my junior year, I get my first flunk grade! I went to talk to my teacher about it. I expected her to bawl me out, but instead she asked whether something was wrong. That surprised me, so I began to look at things I'd never really thought about before.

1

"Sure, I've always made good grades. But I don't know how I do. I don't really like school; I don't really study and I think I'm a poor reader. I know how you're supposed to read: fast and skim the material and recite it back to yourself. I can't do that. I have to read slowly, but I get what I read—I never read anything over, yet I remember things. But I don't like to read and I never crack a book until I have to! I get good grades mostly because I can get things in class. I'm very good in math—I always get A's—but I never study it. Truly, I never studied at all last year, except for our final history test. Then I got an A. I know if I studied every day, like Alice, grades wouldn't be any problem. But, this year I haven't tried very hard. I don't know why.

"Maybe it's because I worry about my brother. He was here in school last year—but now he's away in the Army. I didn't go around with him an awful lot, but just seeing him in the halls and sitting around at home talking with him and his friends was nice. He and I had to take care of ourselves. Mother was never at home—she's been a legal secretary as long as I can remember—and Dad's an architect. When they *are* at home, we're all busy. I play the piano or teach my dog tricks or practice my ballet lessons. We never have time to talk, and I never read. We've got books around, but nobody read me stories even when I was little, so I just never got interested in reading.

"My parents let us alone. Oh, they do a lot for us—give us music lessons and all we want—but they just don't have time to talk to us. So my brother and I used to talk—and now he's gone. I miss him. I talk to Alice some. She's my best friend, but I don't really understand her and sometimes I'm afraid of her. She expects so much of me—she just takes it for granted

2

that everyone is like her. She's got everything—the world's her oyster. She's always been bright and beautiful and popular and rich and talented. She expects everything, and she gets it. Everything comes easy to her. I guess she thinks life's like that for everyone. So I can't tell her how mixed up and scared I sometimes feel. She might think less of me. Besides, she wouldn't understand.

"It's funny, though! Lots of our friends think Alice and I are just alike. But really, I'm shy and scared lots of times. My brother used to tell me last year to stop going through the halls with my head down. I guess I did, except when I was with Alice. Then I pretended to be very gay—lively, like her. But I wonder lots of times whether people really like me and then I'm afraid to look them in the eye. I don't know why I feel like this because I guess people do like me. They come to me a lot to tell me their troubles. I always listen and pat them on the back and encourage them and they say I help them a lot.

"My brother and I used to talk about things; we'd help one another. But that's only been in the last few years. You know how it is with boys and girls—when they're little, they don't like one another. We fought a lot too. Besides, my parents always liked him better than me, so for a long time, I almost hated him. He always was perfect. Anyhow, Mother never wanted a girl because they're so much bother—and me especially. She never forgave me for embarrassing her at a piano recital when I was eight. I walked off the stage. I just refused to play; I don't know why.

"But when Bud and I got in high school, somehow we got together. We began to like each other and we talked lots. He's the one who persuaded me to try out for cheerleading.

3

You know I made the team this year? I can't tell you what that's meant. It's made a new person of me! People I don't know or ones who never talked to me before stop me in the hall and tell me how good I was at the game Saturday. I appreciate that. I guess Alice just takes that kind of compliment for granted—but me, I'm so thrilled when it happens! It's wonderful; I've never had it happen to me before. Why I even go around this year with my head up! It's made a lot of difference—or maybe I'm just growing up! Mother is always saying, 'I wish you'd grow up.' But I'm not sure I know what growing up means."

Linda says, "Things have been tough lately." The school reports that Linda has been impudent to teachers. What the school does not know is that four months ago Linda was suddenly told by her father, just after her friends had departed from "the best Halloween party I ever had," to pack her bag, because the family was moving away from that city the very next day. Now Linda is an eleventh-grader in the new high school of a small community. She says she can't make many friends here. Her father feels that she has deliberately gotten into a fast gang. Linda says they're the only ones who will talk to her. "You have to have someone to pal around with. You can't eat alone in the school cafeteria." Besides, Linda feels that her teachers and her parents blame her for things that aren't her fault. When this happens, she is too angry and proud to try to explain.

Linda has other worries. Her boy friend lives in the city from which they moved. She hasn't found any boy she especially likes in this school. So she's asking herself, "Should I get serious with him? He'll be going into the Army soon, and then I might lose him. Or should I get a job, and not marry so early? I've always wanted to be a dress buyer." Linda's

4

parents are divorced. She lives with her father and her step-mother. She feels guilty because she seems to get along much better with her stepmother than with her own mother. She fights with her own mother, yet she feels sorry for her because she's had several nervous breakdowns so severe that she's had to spend time in a mental hospital.

Linda says, "I'm growing up. I should be able to solve some of these problems, but I don't know what to do."

Like Patti and Linda, most girls are having experiences which make them seek help in learning how they can understand themselves. "What can I expect of myself? What kind of person am I? How did I 'get this way'? How can I make friends? Why am I not as interested in, and attractive to, boys as other girls are? How can I get along better with my family? How do I decide what to do about marriage or about a job? How will I find the job I am 'fitted for'? How do I decide what I want out of life? What can I believe in?" These are questions to which every girl must learn some answers before she can consider herself grown-up.

What does growing up mean? Growing up is a gradual process. You grow up over a period of years. Physically, you may mature at some time between the ages of ten and seventeen. Your intellectual growth began at least as early in life as you first attached meanings to your daily experiences. Later you symbolized those meanings in language. Your mental curiosity increased. Your stock of information still continues to grow year by year, as you move from one class to another in school. Whether you learn much or little depends, partly, on how much you try to learn. Nevertheless, some growth is inevitable; just the process of living forces you to grow!

You began growing up socially when you discovered other people around you—parents, brothers, sisters, grandparents

—all of whom had their own interests and desires. Then you were old enough to play with other children. Did you fight if they did not give up their toys when you wanted them? Did you pick up your dolls and go home if they would not let you be the mother when you all played house? If you accidentally broke something, did you run away or blame someone else?

Emotionally, you began to form habits when, as an infant, you first discovered that you could force people to pay attention to you by crying or that you could get what you wanted by "making a scene." Some persons act in these childish ways all of their lives. These people are lopsided. In a manner of speaking, one part of them remains infantile. You know the kind of woman who throws a temper tantrum because her husband will not buy her a new dress or take her to the movies; the kind of girl who will not marry because she cannot leave her mother; the girl who just drifts from one job to another because she cannot seem to "get down to work"; the older woman who has no friends because no one can get along with her; the pessimist who has gone sour on the world and cannot find a cheerful thing to say about life. Not a single one of these people is very grown-up emotionally. You will want to learn to understand them, to be tolerant of them, but not to excuse yourself for similar behavior. There are many infants in the world who are no longer in cribs.

How Grown-up Are You?

If people are never completely grown-up but are always growing, how can a girl find out where she stands at the moment in relation to other high school girls? A girl may not even be aware of the fact that in some ways she is be-

6

coming a different person; she seldom knows how grown-up she is at any particular time. She is told, perhaps, that she is now old enough to take certain family responsibilities or to earn some money in her spare time. On the other hand, she may find that she is not considered old enough to choose all her own clothes or to stay out late at parties. This is confusing.

There are, nevertheless, certain guides which may help you to see yourself: Do you keep yourself well and happy? Do you live happily with your family? Do you make friends easily? Are you interested in boys? Are you planning a vocation? Do you take responsibility for getting your schoolwork and household tasks done? Are you interested in people? Do people like to have you around?

Growing up is a gradual process. You will continue to grow—mentally, emotionally, and socially—to the end of your life.

Look at yourself as you pass through the various experiences of one day of your life. Sometimes you agree with virtually every suggestion made to you; sometimes you object to nearly everything that anyone says. You may sometimes play for the center of attention in one of a number of ways—by talking or giggling loudly, by pretending illness, by flying into a rage or sulking, by being the life of the party, by acting sophisticated and blasé—superior to "all this," by being either boy-crazy or "sour grapes" on boys, by protesting loudly that you will not speak to anyone and going off into a corner by yourself, or by trying to plan everything and boss everyone.

On rare occasions your moods may go from the extremes of hilarity to the deepest depression, from self-consciousness, when you are so concerned about what someone may be thinking of you that you stutter and fall over your own feet, to bravado and strutting, by means of which you try to convince yourself that you are perfectly poised. You may be "on top of the world" because a teacher has singled you out for a compliment; again, you may find yourself lonely and a wallflower at the class party. You may thoughtlessly change from a feeling of affection for a girl to one of bitterness that makes you quarrel and say mean things. You may unthinkingly revolt against what your parents or other adults think you should or should not do, yet conform in every detail to what the gang or an older person whom you admire does.

Why do most girls occasionally act in one or more of these childish ways? High school girls are always asking, "What makes me act that way?" At the same time nothing makes a girl angrier than to have an exasperated adult demand impatiently, "Why did you do that?" If the girl only knew, the problem would be easier to solve. She may know, for instance, that she wants to make friends and have a good time. For this she needs clothes and money, poise and self-confidence. She may know that she wants to find a boy whom she can like very much and perhaps someday marry, or that she wants a satisfactory job, or that she wants to get along with the people at home.

Just as a girl's physical development is uneven and does not all occur at the same time, so her emotional development has its ups and downs, and these are very hard to understand. She may say that she wants to "express herself." Yet when she tries to do so, she finds out that there are many sides to her nature—that she has no one "self" to express. She discovers that she is a different person in different places and with different people, that the way she feels and acts depends on what she thinks people think of her or on what they expect of her.

On the other hand, she may say that she wants to develop self-confidence. This problem of gaining self-confidence confronts every girl who is growing up. Each girl wants to believe in herself—that is, she wants to believe that she is attractive and capable, that wherever she goes she can depend on herself, that she "stacks up" well in comparison with other people, that she has something to give that other people appreciate. Yet each girl has doubts about herself at some time or other. The thing to remember is that only through action can we get rid of doubts. A successful—or even an unsuccessful—attempt to *do* something about her doubts will help a person to understand a situation better and therefore feel more confident in handling the next one.

What Is Emotional Maturity?

How does a person act when she is "grown-up"—or "emotionally mature"? The mature person generally has a sense of security, of knowing what is expected of her and what she can do. This sense of security may manifest itself in some of the following patterns of her behavior: She has techniques with which to meet and get along happily with people, including her family and the opposite sex. She is not bowled over by her fears, loves, angers, jealousies, or worries. She is willing to take responsibility, to size things up, make her own decisions, and be either praised or criticized for what she has done. She neither fears nor resents honest criticism. She recognizes and uses her abilities, but she also faces her limitations and admits her mistakes. She faces new situations without undue fear, and she is able, if necessary, to change her ways of acting, even though this change may alter the image of herself that she has had for a long time. She welcomes different points of view and is not narrow or bound by prejudices. In the light of new knowledge, she is able to change her opinion on something that she has long believed. She plans ahead and does not fear the future.

No high school girl could be expected to meet successfully all of these standards because they apply to an adult who has truly grown up. A high school girl is still in the midst of learning what the process of growing up really involves. However, these are goals of emotional maturity against which you can measure your daily behavior. Right now your behavior may sometimes seem not to have much meaning to yourself or to others. You yourself, as well as adults, may be puzzled to know why you behave as you do.

A fourteen-year-old girl, Anne Frank, kept a diary in which she reveals how she felt as she tried to understand herself and to gain self-confidence. Anne and her family were forced into hiding during World War II when the Nazis took over Amsterdam, and Anne kept her diary during these years. You will probably recognize many of your own thoughts about what it feels like to grow up as you read Anne's descriptions of herself, beginning with her earlier school life and her life at home with her family before the war.

A girl in the years of puberty becomes quiet within and begins to think about the wonders that are happening to her.... I think what is happening to me is so wonderful, not only what can be seen on my body, but all that is taking place inside.... Girls of this age don't feel certain of themselves...that they are individuals with ideas, thoughts, habits. After I came here, when I was just fourteen, I began to think about myself sooner than most girls and to know that I am a "person."

I look upon my life, as it were, through a powerful magnifying glass. The sunny life at home, then coming here,— the sudden change, the quarrels, the bickerings. I couldn't understand it, I was taken by surprise, and the only way I could keep up some bearing was by being impertinent.
... my fits of crying, the loneliness, how I slowly began to see all my faults and shortcomings, which are so great. During the day I deliberately talked about anything and everything that was farthest from my thoughts, tried to draw Daddy to me; but couldn't. Alone I had to face the difficult task of changing myself, to stop people's everlasting reproaches, which were so oppressive and which reduced me to such terrible despondency.

11

Things improved slightly in the second half of the year. I became a young woman and was treated more like a grown-up; I started to think . . . and came to the conclusion that the others no longer had the right to throw me about like an india-rubber ball. . . . But one thing that struck me even more was when I realized that even Daddy would never become my confidant over everything. I didn't want to trust anyone but myself any more.

. . . the second great change, my dream . . . . with it I discovered my longing, not for a girl friend, but for a boy friend. I also discovered my inward happiness and my defensive armor of superficiality and gaiety. In due time, I quieted down and discovered my boundless desire for all that is beautiful and good.

Ordinary girls, teen-agers like myself, will think I'm a bit cracked with all my self-pity. Yes, that's what it is. . . . I pour out my heart to you, my diary, then for the rest of the day I'm as impudent, gay, and self-confident as I can be—in order to avoid questions and getting on my own nerves.[1]

Anne, like many other girls, does not always act in a way that can be called emotionally mature, because she is trying out various answers to the question "How can I gain security?" She usually calls it "self-confidence" instead of "security." Her behavior is her means of trying in various ways, bungling and assured, to meet life as it comes, to develop a personality or a "self" upon which she can depend. Only as she honestly and thoughtfully faces her problems day by day, as she tries out her various abilities, does she find out what she can do and how much she can do. Thus she

---

[1] Indented selections are from: *ANNE FRANK: The Diary of a Young Girl*, by Anne Frank. Copyright 1952 by Otto H. Frank. Copyright 1952 by the American Jewish Committee, reprinted by permission of Doubleday and Company, Inc.

discovers that it is fun to accomplish something and to have responsibility. She learns from her mistakes. She gets a glow out of something she can do well. She learns to get along with people and to like them. She gains satisfaction from the knowledge that they like her. A result of her experimentation is that she begins to know herself; she begins to gain self-confidence.

When a girl can look at herself honestly, as Anne did, see her limitations, yet believe in herself with all her being; when she is able to think straight, because she is willing to face facts and to take the consequences of her mistakes; when she is able to recognize her abilities; when she ceases to fear her limitations; when she can look at her failures and not be ashamed but know that they have taught her valuable lessons—then she can straighten her shoulders, lift up her head, look at the world, and say: "I can face life squarely, no matter what it may bring. No failures can make me retreat. No successes can throw me off balance. I love life; I am able to live it."

When a girl has had difficulties and faced them, made mistakes and overcome them, she knows what it means when she says, "I can take it." She has not run away, nor has she sat down on the job and cried that she was "licked." When she has achieved these goals, then she can live happily with other people and make her contribution to the world. This is what psychologists call the *gaining of security*.

As a girl gains security, she becomes less important to herself; she becomes concerned about what is happening to other people and to the world. She grows from *egocentricity*—that is, from thinking that the world must revolve around her and do as she desires—to *socialization*. In other words, she grows from self-centeredness to world-mindedness by learning to put her own desires to one side when there is a conflict between her own good and that of other people.

There Is Only One of You

As Georgia O'Keeffe, the artist, said, "You decide on the kind of person you want to be and then you get at it. It's like a habit of neatness." Martha Graham, the dancer, describes the process of making yourself what you are in these words: "There are two areas you have to embark upon. One is the cultivation of *the craft* in which you are working. The other is that something that is—and has to remain—entirely with you—this is the cultivation of *the being* from which whatever there is to say comes. It just doesn't come from out of nowhere. . . . It costs a great deal of effort and a great deal of time—but—the main thing always is the fact that there is only one of you in the world—just one! . . . They say every snowflake is different. I can well believe it. But you are unique, and if that uniqueness is not fulfilled, then something has been lost. Ambition is not enough, necessity is everything. . . . I have always loved St. John Perse for giving me this line which is in one of his poems: 'We have so little time to be born to this instant.'" And some teen-agers cynically ask, "Are the people around us really alive? Do they know what it's all about?" [1]

What *is* it all about? Mature teen-agers have said: "Proving yourself and getting somewhere are the most important jobs we have—it's 'in' to be an individual and not be afraid to think about and talk about serious questions. Life's not just

[1] Martha Graham, "How I Became a Dancer," *Saturday Review,* Aug. 28, 1965, p. 54.

a matter of 'going along,' getting married, having a good job and raising kids! It's learning to live so you mean something!" Or what Martha Graham calls "cultivation of the being."

How does a girl cultivate herself? Many girls worry about themselves; in fact, some are so concerned over "me, me, me" that they are unable to get out of the rut of self. Most teenagers, however, are idealistic, generous, and eager to give of themselves—but they don't know how. To fulfill her uniqueness, a girl needs to find a way to move from self-centeredness.

One way is to find out what you are good *for;* this involves knowing who you are and what you are good *at.* It is hard for a girl to know herself. Yet it can be done; the next chapters emphasize the *how.* Suppose we begin with knowledge of a girl's physical self. It may seem easy to secure. From looking in a mirror, one reasons, a girl can catalog her attributes. But what if her mirror is a relentless critic? It can threaten her self-image—or it can encourage her to make the most of herself!

Knowledge of her mind is even harder to secure. A girl does not usually know what she *really* is able or unable to do because she rarely uses the limit of her potential ability. Nor is she aware of how expertly or inefficiently her mind approaches problems and resolves them because she has not found out how she learns best—what motivates her to make her either keep on trying or give up.

Knowledge of her emotional self is most difficult for a girl to gain. She may learn to recognize when she feels angry, frightened, joyful, anxious, or jealous, but if the reasons for this behavior are a mystery to her, she may judge herself harshly as an inferior person. To know her own worth and to

15

judge herself accurately, she must learn to understand her behavior as *her unique way of coping* with her world.

As a girl finds out who she is and what she can do, she also discovers what she cannot do. She accepts her limitations as well as her assets as parts of her unique self. Between *knowing* herself and *accepting* herself, a girl often finds that she must take a giant step; she must have the courage to live with her inadequacies and the honesty to appreciate what she is good *at!*

Achievement and accomplishment in a wisely chosen vocational field are another part of self-acceptance. A girl must know *what she can do*. But this phrase has a broader aspect than the vocational meaning alone.

Even after a girl has embarked on her "craft," as Martha Graham calls it, she must continue to "cultivate" her uniqueness. This means knowing, not only what you as an individual and as a worker are good *at*, but also what you are good *for*. What have you to contribute in your relationships with people, in pursuit of ideas, in understanding what is important in life?

To answer important questions like "Who am I? What am I good for? What have I to give?" a girl must move from *accepting* herself to *becoming* herself. She must begin, step by step, to learn to make the contributions she alone can make. This is a goal toward which you continue to work all your life. One might say that, in seeking to fulfill your uniqueness, you are embarking on a lonely journey toward self-realization—"You decide on the kind of person you want to be and then you get at it."

CHAPTER TWO

Gaining Self-confidence

GIRLS ALL have a longing for security, a desire for self-confidence. Every girl believes in her own potentialities enough to wonder sometimes, "Why do others accomplish more than I?" or "How can she do so many things?" or "Why does she go over better with people than I do?" In other words, "What makes that girl different from me?"

Girls obviously differ in height, weight, color of eyes, ability to do academic work, ability to do things with their hands, and so on. Just as girls differ in physical ways and in certain abilities, so they differ in personality traits, in their individual feelings of security, and in their ability to get along with people. Each girl will always be different in many ways from all other girls, no matter how much she attempts to change herself. Each has her own special problems to meet, her own inadequacies to accept, as well as her own abilities to develop.

"But people are always applying measuring sticks to me. They are always comparing my accomplishments and weaknesses with those of someone else," one girl complains. This fact, instead of being frightening, should be a challenge. Because of a realization that people do make such comparisons, a girl can develop the habit of making them for herself. Like Anne Frank, she can try honestly to see herself in relation to other people. Mature girls try to discover and to face their own inadequacies and their own faults, as well as to find and to make the most of their particular potentialities.

We All Have Difficulties

Any girl who is honest with herself realizes, of course, that she has physical, mental, and emotional limitations. Since her inheritance comes from both her father and her mother, she may have opposing or conflicting characteristics and inclinations. In addition, she may have learned from her two parents different or even opposite ways of looking at things. Therefore, it may be difficult for her to make certain kinds of decisions; she may seem to have conflicting "pulls" or loyalties within herself. However, this doesn't mean that she may excuse herself for failure in a difficult situation by saying, for example, that she does not have the "brains" to meet the problem, that her parents are not smart and so she is not smart. The girl who makes alibis like this for herself has not yet learned that the kind of "smartness" that enables a girl to go through life as a well-adjusted person must be acquired by each girl individually. No one is born with this ability; each person is born only with a *capacity* to learn. The level of scholarship that a girl has the capacity to achieve can be measured fairly accurately, but the range of things that she will learn in order to become a happy, well-adjusted individual is determined largely by her own efforts.

You may attempt to blame your ancestors for what you are; you may perhaps accuse your parents of bringing you up wrong. Yet you have to admit that you yourself are in many ways responsible for what you have become. And, whether you recognize it or not, it is you yourself who must decide day by day whether to do this or that, whether to go this way or that. As you grow up, you manage your own life more and more. Of course, you and your friends, as individuals, vary in the ways you manage your lives. Some of you let yourselves be slipshod and easygoing. Some of you fool yourselves; instead of facing today, you retreat to the past or dream about the future. Some of you do not try to learn from your mistakes. Instead, you spend your energy trying to justify yourself. Others of you accept your responsibilities, deal with today's problems, stick to a job and struggle through until it is finished.

Let us admit that we all have limitations. On the other hand, let us remember that every infant is born a bundle of possibilities. Probably no individual has ever fully developed all her possibilities. She still has at any stage of her life the resources for great additional personality growth if she will take advantage of opportunities offered her. The kind of person that any one of us becomes, therefore, is determined to a large extent by such factors as these: the use that we make of our abilities, the honesty with which we face our difficulties, the degree to which we either overcome or compensate for our weaknesses, the success with which we learn to meet and to get along with people—in other words, by the pattern that we make out of all our experiences.

19

Naturally, many difficulties stand in everyone's way—difficulties that may seem so serious as to be frightening. The way in which you meet these difficulties will determine the sort of person that you will become. If you learn early in life to face difficulties courageously, no one problem can ever completely overwhelm you. The real test comes when a girl is exposed to any extreme, when she suffers too much humiliation or failure, or when she meets too much success. How will *you* act when you are cornered or when you are overpraised?

Let us consider a few of the difficulties confronting some girls:

Mary is a plain-looking girl. Her mother says that she cannot see why Mary is so plain when the rest of her children are pretty.

Jane has a hard time getting her lessons. Sometimes people laugh when she makes a mistake in class.

Flo's father earns very little. She has no spending money and very few clothes of the sort that other girls have.

Dorothy is in the honor society and is president of one of the largest girls' clubs in school. Yet, when the club gives a dance, she seldom is asked to dance. When the boys do ask her, she is afraid that it is only because they think they should. As for being "rushed," that is beyond her experience.

Sue worked very hard on the yearbook and did so well that everyone thought that she would be the editor this year, but someone else was elected.

Marguerite is in every activity in school and she is a good student. But she cannot be persuaded to attend class dances and parties. She says that she cannot think of anything to talk about.

You can probably think of many other problems that girls must meet. No one would, of course, expect to find a high school girl anywhere who feels completely sure of herself everywhere she goes or in everything that she does. Sometimes, however, a girl has too much of the feeling that she'll never amount to anything. She has so much of it that she almost never feels "natural"; she is always in torment, asking herself, "Are they talking about me? Don't they think I can do it? Maybe they're right. Maybe I can't do anything. Maybe I don't deserve their confidence." If a girl constantly spends her energies in fighting her doubts of herself, she begins to feel inferior.

The basis of this feeling of inadequacy may be physical. Perhaps it is extreme tallness or shortness, protruding teeth, defective speech or hearing, or even a pug nose. Many girls are sensitive about a poor complexion or a scar.

There are other causes, besides physical ones, for a feeling of inadequacy. A girl may have grown up in a family and a neighborhood where there were no boys. As a result, she does not know how to make friends with boys. There may not be many guests in her home, so that she has not had much opportunity to practice conventional good manners; she feels that she does not know how to meet people or to carry on an ordinary conversation. Perhaps she has had to work after school, and consequently it has been difficult for her to get to know many boys and girls of her own age. Her family may believe that women do not need any education beyond high school; so they cannot understand why she wants to have further schooling. Disadvantages of this sort can be real handicaps to a girl as she tries to meet and over-come her difficulties.

Immature Ways of Responding to Difficulties

How do girls behave when they face such difficulties? Let us observe how some high school girls might behave in a club meeting. One girl is criticizing everything done by other persons, including the adults in the group. Another is alternately boasting about herself and disparaging herself. She seems particularly to delight in telling girls how "dumb" she is, hoping of course that they will assure her that she is brilliant. Another girl attempts to hold the attention of the group by telling jokes that no one else thinks are funny. Still another girl relates all the mean things she can think of about the girl who has the class office that she wanted. There is a girl who enjoys bossing everyone. Another has an attack of the giggles as soon as anyone whom she does not like begins talking in the meeting. Still another will speak to no one except the girls who have the reputation of being in "the" group in school. There is a girl who just sits, saying nothing, but virtually worshiping the president of the club. Another girl, who dresses in extreme style, flashes jewelry of all kinds, uses too much make-up, and has her fingernails covered with a deep red polish, often likes to come late. She sits by herself, loftily silent and scornful. That girl in the front row is always on her feet objecting to every suggestion which anyone else makes, calling girls "dumb" when they oppose her suggestions.

Why do some girls behave in these ways? A girl does not do such things maliciously, or even deliberately. She is trying to discover her own personality. She is groping for means by which to meet her difficulties and to gain the admiration we all need. She has hit upon a particular scheme of behavior, perhaps because it worked before—at home or in her earlier school life. If a certain way of behaving once gets a girl what she wants, she may tend to repeat it. Such behavior is only an attempt to get what you want, or what you think you want, and a means of escaping what you do not like.

Some of the girls just described are meeting their difficulties by giving in. They feel that they are "licked" and that they can never be as good as other people. They have a secret suspicion that they can never amount to anything. They adopt a scheme of behavior, such as talking loudly, doing the thing which will attract the most attention, or blaming someone else for their failures in the hope that no one will suspect how they really feel.

Other girls are refusing entirely to look at the fact that they have limitations. They are failing to make any effort to take an active part in life. They are not developing the abilities that they have. They are denying the real world around them and turning to an unreal world of their own, to daydreams in which they can picture themselves as always successful. There are two things that all these girls have in common: a vague awareness of a handicap and an accompanying feeling of inadequacy.

As has been said, everyone has both strong points and weak points. Why do many girls develop feelings of inadequacy because of their handicaps, as these girls just described have done? Sometimes a girl feels inadequate because she *thinks* that she has been given "a raw deal," that she has been cheated, sometimes because she *thinks* that she is not as good as someone else. Some girls feel inadequate because

23

they have been pointed out with scorn or pity, or compared, to their disadvantage, with other people. Whether the handicaps of the girls whose behavior has been described are real or imagined, each really feels that she is not so good as someone else, and each girl has developed a method of behaving that she thinks will bolster her up in the opinion of others. She wants people to like her, but her behavior creates an impression just the opposite of that which she wishes to create.

One tragedy of an inferiority feeling is that the handicap which the girl thinks is there may be only imagined. Yet, if she acts as if it were there, she puts up a barrier between herself and other people—a barrier that makes it impossible for others to reach her. Her behavior, resulting from a feeling of inadequacy, repels and antagonizes people. Thus they dislike and avoid such a girl. This means more sorrow, more of a feeling of failure. And so it goes in a vicious circle; if a girl is *too* conscious of her handicaps, she may distort and irreparably damage her whole life.

The Grown-up Way

What should you do if you find that you do have some handicap—as practically everyone does? Face it and begin planning how you can overcome it. If you face a handicap, it can become a real advantage because you will put forth extra effort to overcome it. Girls who go through life too well satisfied with themselves do not utilize this extra drive. If there is a difficulty in your life that seems to be insurmountable and that might place you permanently at a disadvantage with other girls, face the actual situation. Already you may have had your self-confidence shaken or your feelings terribly hurt because you were made to believe that you are an inferior person. Take stock of your resources and your abilities. Begin picking up the pieces and rebuilding. Instead of trying to be superior where you cannot be and feeling humiliated because you fail, make a list of the things that you can do. Then begin to get your satisfaction by actual achievement.

Do you know the story of Clara Barton? She spent several years of her childhood in a sickroom, nursing a crippled brother. As a result of this experience, she became shy, retiring, and afraid of people. Since she recognized the fact that such an attitude might handicap her later in life, she worked to overcome this difficulty, and she succeeded. With her experience in nursing as a background, she founded the American Red Cross and, in connection with her work, traveled all over the world working with people.

As a result of illness, Helen Keller became blind and deaf when she was two years old. Yet she graduated from college, was well known as a writer, traveled the world in the interest of the handicapped—even made a movie and had one made about her. Eleanor Roosevelt, as a girl, was considered homely and painfully shy. She became a woman whose genuine concern for other people was so widespread and sincere that she was known as the "First Lady of the World."

Therefore, if you have a handicap, work to overcome it. Some of the world's geniuses have accomplished great things because of the extra effort they were forced, by a handicap, to put forth. Success is partly a matter of how much you want a thing and how hard and constantly you will work to get it. You may use your handicap to excuse yourself for being lazy and quitting or for being a coward and running away. On the other hand, your handicap can furnish the drive that makes you put forth extra effort. Thus you may succeed in a task where others, who have not learned to work hard, may fail.

Know your limitations. You must not stake everything on trying to overcome any one particular handicap. By all means make the most of what you have and of what you can do, but do not be discouraged because some things are forever beyond you. Plainly, a girl who is lame should not expect to win a race or a girl who is homely a beauty contest. However, life consists of more than races and beauty contests. You may be handicapped in some way, but only in reference to that one thing. If the ability to do what you are handicapped in doing were the only way to achieve anything of value in life, you might feel discouraged. In reality, there are many ways of achieving success and satisfaction in living. Be careful not to overvalue what you cannot have.

There are some things that you cannot overcome—such as being nearsighted or being very tall—just as there are things that some girls will never be able to do in school or in a job. If you find that you are unhappy in a particular subject in school because you are unfitted to be taking it, admit it and change to something more in your line. Do not make yourself a failure by trying to live up to impossible standards. Be honest with yourself about your limitations. Then you will not need to dislike other people if they persistently remind you of your handicaps. You will already know your limitations, they will no longer hurt you, and you can spend your time working to excel at something else.

Undoubtedly there will frequently come times in your life when you will need to say to yourself honestly and thoughtfully, "Here is a thing that I cannot do. Then I'll leave it to someone else who may do it better than I. I'm not supposed to be able to do everything. But here is something else that I can do. I'll begin right now to prove to myself that I can."

Remember, too, that the inferiority you fear may be only an imagined one. It may be that people have, in a manner of speaking, dinned it into your ears. It may be true that you are not so smart or so pretty as your sister. Possibly you do not have such good manners or are not so cultured as some of the other girls. This does not mean that you are inferior as a person. Be fair to yourself. Do not exaggerate your poor qualities because others remind you of them. Hold up your head! But do not excuse yourself.

Discover your abilities. Work at what you can improve, and substitute something else for whatever you cannot change for the better. Substituting something else for what you cannot change is called *compensation*. Perhaps you can overcome a handicap directly; on the other hand, you may need to do it indirectly, by substituting something different for that which you cannot do. Do not, for instance, feel sorry for yourself because you have to wear glasses and cannot make the basketball team. Perhaps one of the players on the team wishes that she could write as good stories for the yearbook as you do. Capitalize on your assets and your own abilities. If you are not particularly beautiful, do not despair. The world's most charming, glamorous women are not necessarily beautiful women. Learn what you can about suitable make-up and clothes to call attention to your attractive qualities. Bend your energy toward developing the kind of disposition that will make everyone like you. If you cannot

27

make the best grades, do not weep about it. Try out for the class play or the swimming team, play hockey, or learn figure skating. Your life is not ruined by your limitations unless you allow yourself to be defeated.

However, you must not make the mistake of trying to substitute something that is too hard or impossible for you to do. Give yourself a chance at success. If you fail too often, your sense of inferiority becomes too great. Many high school girls fail because they try to do too many things at once. They want to be in everything; they try out for everything. In school, they get on teams, join clubs, rush from one activity to another. Outside school, they belong to church organizations and carry responsibilities at home. In addition, of course, they are trying to keep up their schoolwork. It is inevitable, then, that they will fail somewhere, that they will have a feeling of futility, a sense of not having accomplished anything or of not getting anywhere.

Constant activity, dabbling in everything, does not build up self-confidence. It is wiser to begin at some one thing at which you have a fair chance of success. Discharge each smaller responsibility as it is given you. When you have promised to undertake something, see it through and do it well. Then you will be considered a dependable person, and your worth will be recognized. When you receive greater honors and responsibilities, you will be more likely to meet them creditably, because you will have learned how to face each smaller problem as it comes. You will be able to face your experiences with confidence, because you know what you can do.

Your failures give you opportunities to learn. Instead of saying, "Someone had it in for me, I didn't get the breaks," "It wasn't fair," "I didn't know what to do," examine your

Looking your best adds to your self-confidence. Experiment with various styles to find out which are most becoming to you.

problem. If it grows out of an experience too difficult for you to handle alone, talk it over with an older friend, a teacher, or someone in whom you have confidence, someone who will understand and who can help you. If you do not know why you failed, if you feel only that something held you back, it may be because some past experiences have built up in you a feeling of inferiority. An adult friend whom you trust may be able to help you understand the significance of these past experiences which have hurt you. If, together, you should decide that you need even further help or that you need professional help, you can go to a trained social worker, a physician, or a psychiatrist. Ask your adult friend or your school counselor to refer you to a reputable person. You will be happier if you will always talk out your problems with someone. Do not break your heart brooding over them alone.

It is difficult to put a bitter experience into words. The deeper the hurt, the more you will shrink from discussing it, because even in thinking about it there is much emotion—perhaps fear, possibly shame. However, when you realize that what you really fear is being hurt again, you can deal more intelligently with that fear. For example, when you see that it is difficult for you to get along with people, not because you are an inferior person, but because at home you have been made fun of, humiliated, or ignored, you can see the situation for what it really is. Too often, when you feel that you cannot get along with people, you fool yourself into thinking that you would rather read or be alone than be with people. Do not run away from a difficult situation in this fashion. Instead, examine the situation. Look back on your experience, and find out why you feel the way you do. Then, with the help of an understanding adult to assist you in taking the first steps, you can begin to build up different feelings and attitudes.

Develop your assets. If you think that you have failed because you did not know what to do or how to do it—perhaps you could not think of anything to say at a party, could not pass an exam, or could not dance—then make up your mind to do something about these inadequacies. If you are interested in becoming a good conversationalist, learn how to talk. If you want to be a good dancer, learn to dance. If you want to be successful in school, learn to study. Do not try to tell people that your grades are poor because you are not interested in grades or that you do not like parties and dances and that is why you remain at home.

Begin to learn the things that you need to know in order to use to the best advantage the abilities which you possess. Develop your assets. This may mean that you should practice dancing, practice studying, or practice talking. No skill is ever learned without being practiced. You must give the time necessary for such practice. You must choose to do such practice rather than to do something else.

Always in life you must make choices if you are to accomplish anything. You must focus your efforts on the things that you consider worthwhile. Some people call this "discipline." It is really *practice*. This kind of practice is effective because you have tied up your efforts to something that you want to learn or want to be. If you desire to be a teacher, for example, you give up your idea of being a nurse, and you work, practice, and put effort into learning to be a teacher. You do not begrudge the time that you spend on the practice, the discipline. There is no self-denial in your giving up pleasures for work that you really want to do. You choose it because you want it. You have your efforts focused on a goal. This is the way to succeed.

A girl was leaving her teacher after her last lesson in swimming. "Well," she said, "I know how to breathe, how to float, how to do a fairly good backstroke and a fairly good crawl. I can swim here in the pool, but I would never attempt to go in the ocean or to swim where anyone was watching me."

The teacher answered, "What you need to do is to practice

those strokes which you know that you can do until they become a part of you. Then, whenever and wherever you get into the water, you will begin doing them automatically. You will forget that there are people around you."

Two years later the girl won a swimming meet at a beach. She succeeded because she had worked. She had practiced; she had gained self-confidence by her application of the simple principles that she had learned in her first swimming lessons. If the girl had entered a meet before she had gained sufficient skill and confidence, she would have failed.

It is the same in other realms of life. As you practice some new skill, you gain confidence in yourself. Gradually you gain more and more skill and more and more self-confidence. Do not try to change your habits and attitudes too quickly. You can get rid of a fear of failure only by replacing fear with confidence, and that takes time. But do begin, practice a new skill, and you will find that you progress.

Learn to do something by actually doing it. When a difficulty confronts you, utilize every opportunity that is given you to meet it, and try to adjust yourself to it in the best possible manner. Then you need never fool yourself about yourself.

The grown-up way to act in the face of difficulties and failures, the way to conquer a feeling of inadequacy, is to face reality. Use your mistakes as learning points in the game instead of as excuses to run away or to feel guilty, inferior, or licked. You will get nowhere by running. You certainly will get nowhere if you sit. Your attitude should always be: "I will take my defeats as well as my victories as part of the game of life. Then nothing and no one can keep me down permanently. I will not go off by myself to brood over

my mistakes and failures; I will talk them over with someone. I will always examine them for what I can learn from
them. I will put into action what I have learned."

If you respond in this manner to whatever life may bring,
you will find a great many satisfactions. It is fun to discover
that you can meet a situation, that you can take responsibility, that you can do things. It is interesting to find out
what was the matter when you failed. If, in addition, you
talk over both your successes and your failures with someone who understands, you will develop the ability to see
things in perspective in your life.

A sense of perspective helps you to see, for instance, that
the whole world is not changed because today you failed that
examination or did not get the lead in the operetta. Nor is
your failure in that one particular situation a measure of
what you can do as a person. At present, you may see nothing but despair, but if you will pick up the pieces and try
again, your point of view will change.

Now, suppose that you have taken your courage in your
two hands and are ready to begin rebuilding. You soon find
that there are many things that you do not know. To meet
every situation in life with confidence requires skill and
some very special knowledge. You will want to set out to
gain both. A clever girl constantly looks around for new
things to learn. You might need to know more about how to
keep healthy, how to choose clothes that are right for you,
how to study, how to be a gracious hostess, how to carry on
a conversation with girls, boys, or adults, how to behave at
a formal dinner, how to dance, play tennis, swim, or do any
of the other things that your crowd does. The more of these
abilities that you can develop, the more things that you can

become interested in and can talk about, the more self-confidence you will have.

You do not, however, learn all these things at once, just as you do not grow up all at once. Moreover, you do not learn them by staying at home and wishing that you had all the knowledge you need. You must practice each new skill. At first your efforts may be awkward and bungling. You may make all kinds of social blunders. You may wear the wrong kind of clothes for a certain occasion. You may sometimes be tactless in your relationships with people. Most of us begin that way. Do not be afraid when people tell you that you did something wrong. Listen and learn. Then try again.

Be attractive. Suppose you look first at your clothes. Probably you cannot have as much money to spend on them as you would like to have. Your first consideration in buying clothes may have to be their practicality; you may not be able to choose them for their appearance alone. Or perhaps you design and make your own clothes. In any case, study your wardrobe intelligently, keep an inventory of the things in it, then shop slowly and carefully for things that will harmonize with whatever clothes you already possess. Your wardrobe should not be a rainbow. Have your coats, hats, dresses, shoes, purses, gloves, jewelry, and other accessories all in harmony with a basic color that you have chosen because you know it is becoming to you. Do not indulge in "high style" for itself alone. Remember, "the latest" may not always be most becoming to you! Wear simple, chic clothes —clothes that are right for *you*.

You can do a great deal to develop your own sense of good taste in style if you keep a style scrapbook. Cut out pictures of dresses, coats, and suits that you consider in good taste.

34

Collect with them pictures of accessories that "fit." Try different color combinations so that you may discover those which are becoming to you. Do not overdo the amount of color in your accessories. Go to the library regularly to look at good fashion magazines; check your own developing "clothes sense" against the best that you can find.

If you need further information about selecting and buying clothes, read some good books on the subject. There is always the possibility, too, that you might secure advice from the teacher of clothing at your school. You might gain valuable suggestions from the art teacher, from programs given in your club, or from a class in school. You could also invite a well-informed stylist from some department store to come to a club or class meeting and discuss with your group the selection of a wardrobe suitable for a high school girl and not too expensive.

If you select your clothes only after you have studied carefully the kinds that are best for you and if you always keep them in excellent condition, you will do a great deal to bolster up your self-confidence, because you will know that you are looking your best. Do not scorn good-looking clothes or allow yourself to dress carelessly. Make yourself look as attractive as you can.

However, there is more to physical attractiveness than clothes. Careful grooming is very important. If you are in such a hurry to get out on a date that you do not take a bath, use a deodorant, brush your teeth, and arrange your hair attractively, not even good-looking clothes can save the situation.

Again, the handsomest clothes will be a total loss if you have not developed good posture. Ask your doctor or health education teacher at school to give you exercises or to recommend sports that will improve your posture, if you need help of this kind. Perhaps you slump and let your feet drag because you think that you cannot look the world in the face. If so, the very act of pulling yourself to your full height, keeping your chin up, and walking with a springy step will reinforce that lagging self-confidence.

Keep healthy. Then there is the whole question of health. Keeping healthy is a social responsibility and is invaluable to personal attractiveness. In order to take intelligent care of your health, you need knowledge about the functioning of your body, about proper diet, exercise, and sleep. You need prompt medical treatment when you are ill, and you need to have a good health examination at least once a year.

Care of your body will give you a large measure of control over forces which might otherwise injure your physical and mental health. Physical health and mental health are closely related. When you are not well, your efficiency is impaired. As a result, your self-confidence is threatened because you cannot do your work well. If you have no pep and feel too listless to take part enthusiastically in games and dancing at a party, you cannot expect to have a good time. It is very generally conceded that often when you have the blues about yourself, you are merely tired and need sleep or are hungry and need a good meal. When you feel bored, you may need exercise. In cases such as these, it is much wiser to take care of your needs than to sit down and get someone to join you in a good cry.

Learn how to study. Good study habits can, in many cases, do wonders to help you improve your schoolwork and build up your confidence in your abilities. Ask your teacher or school reading specialist, who has the necessary knowledge, to help you find out what your difficulties are and how you can correct them. Begin helping yourself by answering these questions: What do you do when you study? Do you go off by yourself, away from radio, television, and conversation? Do you give yourself a chance to concentrate?

One effective method of study is to study factual material intensively for short periods scattered over many hours and alternate these short periods with longer ones in which you study material that demands understanding and application of principles and generalizations. Do you plan your study so that you know how many hours each subject requires, then divide your time so that you do not neglect the difficult or disliked subject? Do you study at regular hours daily— or delay all studying as long as possible and then attempt to cram?

Do you attempt first to gain a general impression of an assignment, to discover the unifying ideas in it? Do you outline the assignment and then ask yourself questions about it, pretending that you are taking an examination on it or that you are preparing to teach it? You might even test what you have learned by trying out some part of the assignment on a member of the family. Do you know how to read accurately and rapidly? Do you get the most out of your reading? Or do you just sit with a book in front of you, wishing that you could learn to concentrate? If, in your studying, you have developed learning skills, then you need have no fear of examinations. The questions that you are asked will probably be no more difficult than those that you asked yourself as you studied. You can, therefore, become absorbed in answering your examination questions instead of in wondering whether you will pass or why your stomach feels so queer.

Improve your social know-how. How can you learn to feel adequate in a social situation? When you attend a party, do you run to the nearest corner in the room and hope that you will not be asked to meet any new people, because you cannot think of anything to say to them? Or do you persuade yourself that you will not attend another party, that you do not like parties, when the truth is that you feel uncomfortable because you do not know how to introduce people? If you feel that your lack of social graces handicaps you with your friends, find a good etiquette book in a library. Refer to it whenever you think of something that you do not know how to do correctly. Try out your new social graces and courtesies on your family and on your friends. Remember, too, that courtesy, in the last analysis, is consideration of other people. If you have forgotten what the book says is the correct thing to do, ask yourself what the kind thing would be, and do that. If you can practice this kind of courtesy, your friends will look forward to having you around at parties, because you can always be depended upon to help make other people feel comfortable.

Where will you learn good table manners? You acquire them only by practice. You can learn to balance a teacup and spoon as you carry on a conversation if you try doing it at home. Stand in front of a mirror and practice someday —when there is no one in the house to tease you for doing it. If you want to feel comfortable at a formal dinner, study the settings given in an etiquette book, and practice the

38

You will grow in self-confidence as you improve your social know-how. Practice at home with your family.

procedures that the book describes as correct behavior. In addition, develop the habit, when you are at the family table or even when you "eat off the pantry shelf," of using the manners that you expect to use at the next club tea or dinner party. If you practice your best table manners every day, you will not have to worry about them on special occasions.

If you are to feel adequate in a social situation, it will help you a great deal to be a good conversationalist. How can you learn to talk to people? Remember, you are not expected to do all the talking! If you are wise, you will listen before you talk. If you are interested in your new friends and in their conversation, this fact is conveyed to them by your facial expression and your manner. You will look interested and truly be interested. You will encourage them to talk by asking intelligent questions about things in which they are interested. This is true, whether you are talking to boys or to girls. If you want to be a successful hostess, learn to be a good listener as well as a good talker. Too many people spend most of their time planning what they will say when the other person stops talking. Others, although quiet, slip into inattentive day-dreaming. A good listener is always appreciated.

A pleasing voice and a broad vocabulary, which show that you are interested in many things, are invaluable assets in carrying on a conversation. Know something about sports, travel, plays, books, poetry, television, what is happening in the world and in space. Read the news section of the daily paper; learn something about politics, economics, and diplomacy. Broad interests make it possible for you to talk easily with any new friend. Your date may be much more interested in the coming election than in the latest mystery on TV. In addition to your concern about the interests of your friends, develop a hobby of your own. You are a much more interesting person if you have a subject about which you too can become enthusiastic in your conversation.

As you develop many abilities, as there are more and more things in life that you enjoy doing with other people, more and more things that you can do well, you find that each accomplishment gives you an added feeling of confidence in yourself. How many things can you do now? Can you swim, skate, dance, play a musical instrument, paint? Almost any girl can develop any of these abilities if she will work at it. It is perfectly possible, for instance, to learn to dance, or to improve your dancing, in a class at school, in a club, or by having your friends teach you. When you know the steps, practice. Go out on a dance floor, even if you feel that you are not so good as some of the other dancers. Most couples will be so interested in one another that they will not even notice you. The only way in which you can learn to become a good dancer is to practice dancing. The same would be true of any skill that you might wish to acquire.

Capitalize on your interests and aptitudes. However, if you are to be a well-rounded, interesting person, you will need—as well as skill and knowledge—an ability to see and appreciate beauty wherever it may be found in life—in a beautiful picture, in nature, in knowing and understanding people different from you in race, nationality, and economic status. To develop this ability, you will need to read books that you will enjoy and to see plays that will thrill you. You will want to learn more about the beauty that these things can add to your life. You will need to know people who live beautifully, so that you will want to live as they do. You will need to have an ideal of yourself which you want to achieve.

You will want to give yourself the opportunity to enjoy music, art, dramatics, and literature. The ability to appreciate and to share your appreciation of the arts makes you a more interesting and a finer person. If you can play a musical instrument, if you can draw, act, or write, your confidence in yourself is enhanced through the satisfaction of accom-

41

plishment; here is something more that you can do, something more that you have to contribute in your companionship with others.

Music can mean much to you, no matter what feelings you need to express, no matter what emotions you need to release. Moreover, understanding and enjoying music can give richness to life. Now that so much good music is available on television, radio, and phonograph records, hear it often, and let it contribute new meaning to your life.

If possible, develop the ability to draw or to enjoy various crafts. You will be surprised at what skill you can develop, what satisfaction you gain as you create something yourself, whether it be on paper, in clay, in yarn, or in any of the many other possible media. To have an idea and to watch it grow into form under your own hands is a real thrill and an achievement of which you can be proud.

Suppose you yourself have comparatively little ability to do things with your hands? Then develop an appreciation of art, of beautiful things. Keep one or two lovely things around you—a beautiful lamp, a vase, or a pretty perfume bottle. You may want to build the color scheme of your room around one lovely picture or flowering plant.

Dramatics offers many possibilities. You may be able to write or help to write a play in school, at home, or in a club. You may be able to act in one, either for a large audience or for the smaller audience of the classroom. You may have a chance to act out, as a part in a play, what you may never have an opportunity to be in real life. Such an experience is the beginning of new self-confidence for you, for here is something more that you can do. You may be spurred on to greater efforts. You will find that your achievements in dramatics give you great satisfaction. Perhaps you prefer to see plays or to read as many of them as possible, then talk about them. An increasing number of good plays can be seen on television, and "live" theater is becoming available in more and more communities. Why not organize a theater club? The stage is a subject that fascinates many people; here you have wide range for your imagination. You can learn about stage design, lighting, makeup, life in the theater, and history of the theater. You will never want for something to do if you are interested in dramatics.

Literature, both prose and poetry, offers you a variety of experiences. As you read, characters in books sometimes mean so much to you that they seem like real people. If you try writing, you can create your own characters. In school, many girls have learned to express themselves in both prose and poetry and have a good time doing it. However, if you do not write, you can still find joy in collecting stories or poems which appeal to you. A professor once said, "The appreciation of poetry is in the ability to see a poem, not to write one!" Try seeing poems.

What, then, is a recipe for developing self-confidence? Bring to your life the best that the world has to offer in an appreciation of literature, music, dramatics, art. Be sensitive to the lovely things of life. Recognize and face your difficulties and failures. Discover your abilities. Develop your assets. Take care of your health. Practice your new habits until you achieve success. Acquire skills, interests, and appreciations which will make you an interesting person. As you thus make life richer for yourself, as you also share with others the best that you have to give, you will gain self-confidence and know the full meaning of happiness.

Self-confidence and Versatility

Have you read about someone who can paint, write, ski, play tennis, fly a plane, and even make an impromptu speech? Did your self-confidence drop? Do you envy such people what you consider a special aptitude for versatility? Actually, these people have the same fundamental equipment as you but use it differently. One might say, they use *all* of it. They concentrate completely on each activity of the day. They do not give merely scattered attention; they give all of their faculties. Normal people have the capacity for concentration. Most of us, though, allow ourselves to be distracted by nervousness, preoccupation, noises, or conflicting interests.

If you are absorbed and interested in what you are doing, you concentrate without effort; concentration follows interest. But interest will also follow concentration. If you learn to throw yourself into each job, no matter how distasteful, you become interested once you get started. Get into working position with both body and mind, and see what happens.

The secret of concentration is to keep at it. Most of us welcome interruptions when we are working, or we allow a multiplicity of thoughts, sounds, and smells to distract us. Though your mind is fastened on one thing, you can think of a dozen other things you ought to be doing. Face this fact. You cannot push the worry out of your mind? Answer it, "Yes, that's important, but it must wait until I finish this task. It shall have my full attention next." Then keep your promise. Arnold Bennett describes this process as developing "the power to dictate to the brain its tasks and to insure its obedience."

Everyone has the *power* to learn many things. It is *control* of this power that requires practice. Keep bringing your mind back again and again to what you want it to concentrate on now, and your competing thoughts eventually will give way. Gradually, you will find that you can count on yourself; you are able, at will, to master a task on which you have chosen to concentrate. Thus you learn to do many things well and your self-confidence expands.

In developing versatility, you must concentrate on learning something new and at the same time face your fear of something new. Perhaps you are afraid of new ideas which might lead you to express opinions different from those of your friends. Is honest dissent so dreadful? Albert Einstein, asked for advice to science students, replied: "Spend an hour every day rejecting the ideas of others and thinking things out for yourselves." Try something new; it may not be as fearful a prospect as you thought! Then, having once overcome fear, it is easier next time to face the difficult and untried. Once you have driven your mind to the hard job of thinking, you will find that the human brain, when forced to function, is an amazingly versatile instrument. It has designed cathedrals, spacecraft, skyscrapers, enduring literature, and the Grand Coulee dam! The difficult job is starting, launching a train of thought, then sweating it out!

CHAPTER THREE

Acting Your Age

THERE COMES a time when you are expected to "face the world." To do this you must have confidence in yourself. You must be able to stand on your own feet. The world will show you whatever amount of respect you demand. You must know what you can give and be confident about offering it. If you show a lack of self-respect, this attitude will influence what other people think of you.

In the last chapter we considered some of the immature and mature ways in which girls, in the process of growing up, respond to difficulties. How would such methods of behavior work out in actual situations? Let us look at three girls who are face to face with problems.

Adrian, Bernice, and Caroline

Adrian is a girl who goes through life facing each problem as it comes. Of course she makes mistakes, but afterwards she looks at them to see why she made them. Adrian has had difficulties this year. She says that, ever since she was a little girl, she has wanted to make a career of nursing. She says, "I always made good grades—until this year. When we

47

moved up here, I didn't know anybody in this school, and I didn't know the teachers. I got so I wouldn't recite in class unless I had to, because I might do or say something they thought sounded dumb.

"Also, I made some mistakes when I first came because I didn't know how they do things here. On my first day, at lunch in the cafeteria, I went and sat with a boy who'd been talking to me while we were in line. I didn't know anyone else, and he seemed nice. Everybody gossiped and said I was fast, because at this school it's just understood that boys sit at some tables and girls at others. In our school, we all sat wherever we wanted. Another mistake I made was that at first I went out with different boys—with anyone who asked me at school, at church, or at the community center. At home, we always did that. We went around in gangs and had a swell time. Here you're supposed to go steady with one fellow. You don't have to go steady too long—just a couple of weeks or a month—but while you're going steady, you shouldn't date anybody else.

"Anyhow, because I got started on the wrong foot, I guess I've spent too much time this year trying to prove I wasn't 'different.' You've got to have friends, and that takes time! Other years, after dinner, I'd stay home and study. This year I couldn't. We'd go to ball games or the movies, or watch TV at someone's house. Then when I got home, I was tired, and it was too late to study. I'm worried about it. I really want to get in a good hospital and be a good nurse. But what can I do? I want friends, too!

"I know it's up to me! I have to decide from now on what I really want. Every day I have to choose whether I'll do things that help or whether I'll drift. I guess I just lost my sense of direction this year. It's hard when you start in a new place. You have to spend time learning how people do things. In a way you need to 'sell yourself' to lots of people and find out whether they'll be friends with you. Now I think people like me. At least, the people I care about do. So maybe next year I won't need to spend so much time thinking about what people think about me. Then I can spend more time thinking about what I think of myself!"

By facing her mistakes, Adrian is learning not to repeat them. "Experience" is the name that she gives mistakes. We say that she "profits" by them. All the people she meets and all that she does contribute to her growth. All this experience becomes a part of her. She has a unified personality, she faces life squarely, she gains something from each of her experiences.

Bernice is a girl who finds it harder to face difficulties. She sometimes feels humiliated because she makes mistakes in school. From time to time she is frightened into feelings of inadequacy by her social blunders. She occasionally feels that her mother punishes her unjustly, and then she feels unwanted at home. Instead of looking at situations honestly, she makes excuses, she rages, she blames her mother or her teacher for being unjust. Once in a while she becomes "high hat" and acts superior to everyone in her effort to hide her lack of self-confidence, her fear that she is not so good as she wishes she were.

Bernice needs to be helped to realize that if she confronts her mistakes and limitations, if she does something to build up her confidence, to develop her assets, then those fears may vanish, or she may even discover that she has been making herself unhappy over fears that were, in part, imaginary.

49

As long as she does not confront those fears, she is like the child in the rhyme who cries,

> Yesterday, upon the stair,
> I met a man who wasn't there.
> He wasn't there again today—
> Oh dear, I wish he'd stay away.

Bernice may discover sooner or later, probably with the help of an understanding adult, that the methods of behavior that she has chosen do not work. People can see through her. They know that she is only pretending to have this abundance of self-confidence. They are not even surprised at her bursts of temper, her moodiness, her sudden rages and angers, her seemingly uncontrollable impulses. They know from their own experience that these methods are not the best ways of getting along with people, for they, too, have tried out these schemes and found them wanting. While they were discovering other methods, they also had to pretend that these were satisfactory ones. Then, as they became confident that they could get along with people by the use of the more acceptable ways of behaving, the second-rate methods were gradually discarded. When Bernice has learned that she does not need to pretend, then she will begin to take a few faltering steps forward, although still hanging on to someone's trust in her to give her confidence.

Most girls learn in this fashion—by trial and error—with many successes, many failures. You yourself find some problems easier to face than others; on some difficulties you need more help than on others. The test is not whether you will need help or how fast you will move forward, but whether you will move.

50

Caroline is a girl who refuses to move. She will not face life. She has built a wall between herself and the outside world. She may have begun building it early. She may have been taught that she was better than other people, that she did not need to learn to get along with them, that they must learn to appreciate her. She may have been deeply hurt. She may have a physical handicap, because of which she has allowed a feeling of inadequacy to get the better of her. For any one of a number of reasons, she has grown to physical maturity knowing little or nothing about people and the world around her. She has not learned either how to enjoy or how to talk to people. She is shy, afraid of people, living in a world of her own—daydreaming, brooding, reading, writing, generally by herself. Girls, boys, or adults concerned about her sometimes try to tempt her out of herself. She does not respond; she slinks off. Sometimes she peers cautiously at people as if from around a corner, but she will not come out and face them and run the risk of being hurt. Life's problems are solved for her by others; of life's real experiences she knows nothing. Even though it may not be entirely Caroline's fault, she is, nevertheless, a poorly integrated and very lonely girl.

Why should we discuss in detail these examples of adjustment or lack of adjustment? Because the teen-age years are especially significant in their relationship to later life. The teens are only one stage in this process of growing up, but if a girl is to continue to grow the rest of her life, she must meet successfully the problems which face her while she is a teen-ager.

Growing up is a gradual thing. It takes time—and understanding. Growing up is not just using make-up, wearing a sophisticated hair-do, or having a boy friend. Growing up, as one author says,[1]

> ... is not putting on a lot of stuff from the outside. It's an inside thing—a power that some call intelligence or experience. ... Whatever you call it, it's the thing that mellows people. You ripen under it. You drop off the kid stuff. You don't have to shout so loud to be heard. You don't have to show off so much. You feel all quiet inside. You learn to think. It doesn't matter so much what other folks do or say because you're sure of yourself inside. You know what you are and where you're going.

Why the Girls Behaved as They Did

Naturally, when so many things are happening to a girl all at once—when she is trying to become emotionally independent of her family, when she is thinking about a job, when she is concerned about her success in school and about her friendships with both boys and girls, when she is wondering what life is all about anyway—it is inevitable that she will have periods of emotional strain. She will have some severe difficulties. She will probably meet some failures. There will be times when it is not easy for her to face something at home, at school, with a girl or boy friend. Under the stress of emotion, she may resort to forms of behavior which are, at best, second rate.

Everyone acts badly sometimes. People are such complex beings. Have you ever noticed that pieces of you may do things of which other pieces of you are ashamed? That you act differently as circumstances differ? That you keep trying

[1] Amelia Elizabeth Walden, *Three Loves Has Sandy*, Whittlesey House (McGraw-Hill Book Company, Inc.), New York, 1955, pp. 117–118.

different ways of behaving, different ways of responding to people, until you find one that you think meets your need at the moment? In your desperation, you may use a second-rate response—that is, you may give up, lie down on the job, and consider yourself licked; you may refuse to face your failure; or you may find yourself bragging, being sarcastic, rebelling, or daydreaming.

You use such techniques of behavior only because it is necessary for you to have someone notice you, to have someone be conscious of the fact that you are around, to have someone feel that it is worthwhile to cultivate your acquaintance. You crave recognition; therefore, you exert yourself to gain that recognition by trying out many different ways of behaving. Of course you need the feeling that you are as good as anyone else. Your desire for security demands that you do something to relieve a feeling of inadequacy, but you betray your lack of belief in yourself if you try desperately to be noticed by resorting to unusual behavior in order to make a bid for attention.

However, when you have convinced yourself that you are a worthwhile person, these types of behavior will vanish because you no longer need them. When you are certain that you do count for something, that you will not be scorned or considered inferior because of your limitations, then you no longer resort to unusual behavior to draw people's attention to you. You are secure in the knowledge that if you are called upon to do something, you will have a contribution to make, that if you are asked to take responsibility, you will discharge it creditably. In other words, you will have acquired poise and self-confidence.

Meeting Difficulties Intelligently

Feelings of insecurity and strain are likely to come with all new experiences. Every girl must learn, therefore, to recognize and to deal with these feelings intelligently. Suppose we examine some of the less desirable types of behavior. Then, the next time you find yourself resorting to them, you can jerk yourself up by saying to yourself, "See here, do I want to accept second-rate behavior from myself? What can I do instead?"

The way of behavior that you choose may be the best that you can do under the circumstances, but be sure that you are honest with yourself in deciding that it is. If a girl is habitually shy, for instance, she may argue that the withdrawn, shy girl is also the more sensitive, understanding person. It may be true that such a girl has a great deal to give in the way of understanding other people, yet as long as she withdraws, she is failing to give anything and is of little use to herself or to others. If she were honest with herself, she might recognize that such behavior is merely the path of least resistance and that she is dropping into the habit of doing the easiest thing, just as the girl who habitually has temper tantrums has fallen into the habit of doing the impulsive thing. Habits are merely methods of response acquired by frequent use. Therefore, any given method of response will become a habit if you practice it often enough.

No use crying. Having temper tantrums is certainly a second-rate way of responding to difficulties. What other second-rate responses may a girl resort to when she has not learned to face her problems or has failed to attain her ideals in the world of reality? She may decide that she is "never going to amount to anything anyhow." Probably she expresses this feeling by going into a state of depression, by feeling guilty and overcome with remorse and despair, or by crying. There are many girls and grown people who do nothing more than sit and cry when they have done a wrong to someone or when they are faced with the results of their own mistakes.

However, crying to make people know that you are sorry for your failure or mistake does not make them or you any happier. Have you ever heard anyone express great satisfaction over a broken and contrite heart? Nietzsche, the philosopher, says that remorse or self-punishment is, at best, always a dishonest business. You cannot right a wrong that you have done a person or heal a hurt that you have given by punishing yourself. When you do that, you are just like the three-year-old who had been told not to touch Mother's magazines. He sat tearing them up, page by page, slapping his hands as he did so, and saying, "No, no!"

If a girl continues to punish herself for her mistakes, she is likely to become a failure because she thinks that she deserves only failure, or to lose her friends because she considers herself unworthy of them. It is true that you may not be blamed so severely for the thing you have done if you cry or punish yourself. But it is much fairer to apologize to those you have hurt and then, if you can, to begin doing something at once to right the situation, even if that thing is no more than going in and helping with the dishes.

Talk to someone. On the other hand, a girl may refuse to tell anyone about her failures, refuse even to talk to anyone; she may just get off by herself and brood. Probably she is using this brooding as a means, consciously or unconsciously, of gaining sympathy, attention, and love. You know the kind of girl who habitually gets the blues and wants her mother or someone else to wait on her, to cheer her up, to tell her how much she is loved. If this scheme works once, the girl may try such behavior again and again.

We all need love, but we seldom admit to ourselves that we would use such an infantile method to secure it. We cannot face the humiliation of thinking that people might care for us only because they feel sorry for us. Nevertheless, with some individuals brooding and despondency have become a method of fooling other people into giving them the attention that they crave.

What are some of the problems a girl might brood about? She might be worried because boys do not like her as well as they do other girls, because she does not have as much money as some of her classmates, because she is not as good in athletics as some of her friends, because she cannot earn such good marks as she would like to and feels that she is disappointing her parents.

Brooding is useless, and it can easily become a trap. A girl is confronted with a difficulty. She goes off and broods. No one discovers her and comforts her. She becomes more miserable than ever, because she is sure, then, that no one cares about her. So, instead of becoming more friendly and attractive, instead of managing her allowance better, instead of improving her skill in some sport or doing better in her studies, she grows less capable, less attractive.

Instead of brooding over her problems, she can plan to face and solve them. Ways in which she can do this were discussed in the last chapter. A girl might also try talking out her problems with someone who will be sympathetic.

Discussing a problem helps you to face it and often points the way to a solution. Talking things over also helps you learn to be a thoughtful friend.

Difficulties do not sound nearly so insurmountable after they have been discussed, for two people can usually find solutions for them more easily than can one person struggling with them alone.

Admit your mistakes. There are people who, in place of blaming themselves, blame someone else, or "the world." People imply the latter when they talk of "bearing the burdens" which fate has sent them. Curiously enough, it is generally the people who have failed to live as successful lives as they had wanted to live, or those who feel inferior to others, who say that the world is not a fit place in which to live. You know people who blame their failure to accomplish anything on the fact that their families are always having misfortunes or that someone is always ill. You also know people who are constantly lamenting the fact that they have to work so hard and can never have a good time. These people want to believe that the whole world is sick, in order to convince themselves that they are well.

It does not humiliate one's ego, one's self, nearly so much to blame fate or the world for one's failure as it does to admit one's own inadequacy. People can become bitter, sarcastic, or cynical about the world and the people in it. In reality such people may be expressing their disappointment in themselves, though they don't admit it. It is much healthier, however, to admit one's inadequacy and to begin to work on methods of compensating for it.

It is true that girls may have learned from others this habit of shifting the blame for behavior on someone or something else. Some older person may actually have recommended this method of meeting difficulties. A girl often discovers early in life that if she can prove that someone else is as guilty as she is, her punishment may not be nearly as severe. If she learns no better method of adjustment, this habit may persist; she may spend the rest of her life looking for people on whom she can blame her difficulties and mistakes. For example, when she fails in an examination, she may say that the teacher does not like her. When she has a quarrel with her girl friend, she may claim that the girl friend started it. When she cannot secure a job, she may say it is because she has no pull. When a boy she likes does not ask her to a dance, she may say that another girl told him some lies about her.

When people persist in taking this way out, life becomes very complicated. As they confront more and more difficulties, it becomes more and more necessary for them to blame others for their failures. Instead of looking for someone else to blame when you fail, it is much more intelligent for you to try harder to improve yourself, so that the next time you are confronted with that problem, or a similar one, you will meet it with success. When you feel confident that you can face and solve your own problems, you will find that you no longer need to spend your time looking for someone to whom you can shift the blame for your failures.

Be yourself. Another testimony to your feeling of inadequacy in meeting a situation is given when you assume the pose of superiority. You may pretend a colossal egotism. You may try to go around only with the people who are "in," those whose accomplishments are recognized and whose reputations are secure. Possibly you proudly talk about "my friend so-and-so," who is the most popular boy or girl in school, the most prominent person in town, or someone well known in the country at large. You may even call such a person by his first name when you are in a group on whom you are trying to make an impression, although you would not dare do so in the person's presence.

If you feel that you are socially inferior, you may become "high hat," plan to be seen with no one but "the gang," spend too much money too obviously, dress in extreme style, and conform in every detail to standards set by your crowd, whether you can afford to or not. You behave in these ways in order to bolster your own self-confidence.

If you act like a mature person, you try to discover whatever assets, abilities, or talents you have and make the most of them. Then you can be justly proud of actual accomplishments. When you no longer need to pose as being different from what you really are, you will find that you will be

Compensate for your inadequacies instead of fearing them. Take pleasure in being yourself instead of trying to be somebody else.

happier than you are now, because now you are living under a constant strain of trying to keep up a pretense and fearing that someone will find you out.

Must you be jealous? Reactions of jealousy, hatred, and suspicion are admissions to oneself of a feeling of inadequacy and inferiority in a situation. The jealous girl is always talking in a disparaging way about girls whom she envies for one reason or another. She is always imagining that her friends are slighting her or that her family or her teachers are being unjust to her. She measures everyone by the degree of devotion, even of homage, that they give her. She is haunted by a fear that no one cares for her, yet she pretends that she does not mind whether anyone loves her or not.

Jealousy only drives people away. No one wants to be picked upon constantly. Neither can anyone give love because it is demanded. Moreover, the girl who is really grown-up never expects one person to be as wholly absorbed in her as a mother has to be in a helpless baby. She has learned that it is more fun to care for other people than to be taken care of. She attempts, therefore, to contribute an increasing share to relationships which are meaningful to her. She enjoys the give-and-take in her family circle. She is a thoughtful friend. She utilizes her ability in order to develop techniques which build up her feeling of assurance as she meets various life situations; for example, she learns how to do the best she can in school or how to become a popular guest in the homes of her friends. She thus develops a feeling of security. She no longer needs to be jealous, because her knowledge of her limitations is balanced by a consciousness of her abilities.

Hate is another green-eyed monster. Closely akin to jealousy is hate. This is one of the most dangerous attitudes that a girl can acquire, because it may distort her whole life and lead to eventual breakdown or crime. If a girl has a feeling of hate and does not face it, it gets buried deep inside her. She must find out why she resorts to hatred; she must understand how the process works. Then she will see how dangerous such behavior is and check it. If she does not do so, hate sometimes becomes disguised as love. The girl pretends, in an elaborate fashion, that she likes a person. She may become aware that her pretended love is really hatred only when she

61

finds herself exulting in the fact that that person has met some misfortune, or that some act of hers, which she thought was a kind one, has really caused that person suffering. She may even realize that she had actually been hoping to get revenge on that person.

Does hatred really help a girl to meet her problem? No. Hating blinds her to the real problem. If a girl hates classmates because they have outranked her, because they have hurt or slighted her, by accident or on purpose, because she is, or thinks that she is, inferior to them, what she needs is to have her self-confidence raised. Hating people only lowers her self-esteem and makes other people feel justified in their low estimate of her. Neither is one helped by a desire for revenge. People generally hit back only when they are hurt. When you do mean and petty things, it is generally because you have been hurt and you are trying to get back at someone.

You will be meeting a situation much more intelligently if you face the actual problem. What do you expect to gain by this recourse to hatred—success in school, or the good opinion of your classmates? Find out what it is that you really want, and then ask yourself, "Is there a better way of achieving my purpose?" Then follow the superior method: begin *doing* something to get what you want, instead of hating the people who have already achieved something. You may need to assume a more friendly attitude toward your classmates; you may find it necessary to study harder in school; or you may see that you will have to give up what you want because it is impossible for you to attain it, but you will turn enthusiastically to something else at which you have a greater chance of succeeding.

Trust versus suspicion. A girl may also find herself being chronically suspicious of people. Suspicion is almost as poor an attitude with which to respond to difficulties as is hate. If a girl constantly suspects that the person who hurt her meant to do it, that response can end in only two ways: Either she gets revenge on that person before she is hurt again, or she escapes to protect herself and lives in fear lest that person will hurt her again. The belief may grow that other people are against her, that the world is against her. Having someone merely tell her that her suspicions are unfounded will not convince her. From such attitudes are developed delusions which sometimes lead to acts of violence.

A good way to find out whether or not you are inclined to be suspicious is to think back over the things you say about other people. If you often accuse them of hurting people, of talking in an unkind way about people, of being sneaky, of always having secrets from you, you may be developing a suspicious nature. To be sure, you may have reasons for suspicion about someone; you may have been deeply hurt by a person in whom you placed your trust. It is true that there are people in the world whom you cannot trust. If you want to become mature, you will need to develop understanding and tolerance of people who betray your trust.

However, finding out that some people cannot be trusted does not mean that you need to become suspicious and cynical about everyone. There are many people in this world whom you *can* trust. Approach people with an attitude of confidence instead of with suspicion. You can learn to trust people only by trusting them. What you need is to have a series of actual experiences that will show you that there are people in whom you can confide your deepest desires, with whom you can share your most intimate confidences. If you have several experiences with such people, you will gradually lose your fear and suspicion.

Intelligence versus rebellion. It is sometimes easy for girls to move from these attitudes of jealousy, hate, and suspicion into a desire to rebel. Rebellion is a very dangerous course of action to elect, yet girls occasionally go to great lengths to force people to pay attention to them. They may reason that they have been humiliated, scorned, and made to feel inferior. Therefore, they must demonstrate to themselves and to others that they are not inferior, that they are people to be reckoned with. They may overstep all bounds in order to do this.

Some girls make it difficult for anyone to live with them. At school or in their clubs they attempt to dominate everything; they insist upon their own way everywhere. At home, they bully their younger brothers and sisters; they rebel openly against their parents' authority. They do just the opposite of what they have been asked to do: They wear the kinds of clothes which their parents dislike intensely; they choose friends of whom their parents do not approve; they go to places which have been forbidden; they smoke, drink, or assume a "tough" attitude. Some girls have even resorted to crimes such as stealing, because they thought that they had to do something spectacular in order to secure the attention they wanted.

All this behavior gains a girl nothing except the kind of attention which gives her a poor reputation and loses her the respect of others. This is just the opposite of what she really wants. What she really wants is approval as well as attention; she wants to be accepted and liked. The intelligent way to secure the attention that she wants is to make use of her abilities and to face honestly the difficulties around her. This is the grown-up way. The difference between the two methods can be shown in these two different attitudes toward the same situation: "I can't be president of the club, so I'll try to break it up" and "I can't be president, but I'll do a good job as chairman of this committee."

Why act less grown-up than you are? Jealousy, hatred, and suspicion are ways in which girls may respond to a situation when they give in, when they take the attitude that they have been licked. Another type of response is one that virtually all girls may use sometimes when they refuse even to look at the situation. They will not face the real facts; they retreat into a world of their own making. They will not admit a failure; they try to convince themselves and other people that they did not fail—not they, ever!

How can a girl recognize this type of behavior in herself? Perhaps she becomes like the girl who talks all through the meeting and calls everyone "dumb" who opposes her suggestions. Or, she may be like the girl who has to boss everyone, yet never does any actual work herself. Possibly she is like the girl who is always so busy dashing around, doing the first thing that enters her head, that she never has time to think, and if she makes a mistake, it is because she "has so many things on her mind."

Watch yourself for the times when you talk loudly, affect a loud laugh, use long words, walk or talk in an affected manner, or have your feelings hurt so easily that everyone has to stop and comfort you. Hoist a danger signal when you discover yourself doing such things. This behavior may be an attempt to shock someone into noticing you. If that is true, you become like the five-year-old, yelling, "I will be bad, and I dare you to stop me!"

65

"How good I am!" Likewise, a girl may "get a cause" and begin reforming other people. You know the kind. She can do anything, fix up anybody's difficulties. Reforming others is such a comfortable task. It helps a girl's feeling of inadequacy, because, as she sets out to reform others, she usually assumes that she is better than they are. Besides, she can become so busy seeing other people's shortcomings that she never has time to look at her own. Conversely, a girl may go to the other extreme, become the perfectionist, and demand that everything done must be done perfectly. She announces loudly that she is always right. She goes into a rage if anyone disagrees with her. Such a girl will probably also try to surround herself with inferior people, so that she can show off by contrast.

They know you are bluffing! Remember that it is generally the girl who has done little who has to boast of her accomplishments. It is often the girl who has a comparatively small amount of money who acts as if she had a great deal. It may be the girl who is afraid to carry on a conversation who uses the biggest words. Sometimes the very girl who cannot get a boy friend tells you that her telephone is ringing at all hours of the day and night. Perhaps it is the girl who is ashamed of her home who describes herself as reclining on a chaise lounge in a lavender satin negligee with an ivory telephone next to her.

It may frequently be the girl who has been disappointed in her grades or who has been hurt by her failure to be elected to an office in school who adopts the "sour-grapes" attitude, who becomes sarcastic and bitter, who says that she did not want these things anyway. "They aren't worth going after. Who'd want to be bothered?" she asks. The girl who is not popular may say that she does not want to be popular because popularity would distract her mind—and she wants to become a great opera singer, a famous writer, or a renowned painter. It is sometimes the girl who is unattractive or has no friends among boys who belittles marriage.

In resorting to bluffing, a girl is taking out her anger on herself and on those who scorn her. She owes her aggressiveness to her disappointment in herself. If she were confronted with this fact, she might become panicky. She needs to be helped to see that she cannot gain friends by posing or by showing off. She will merely make girls angry or determined that they will outdo her. She needs, moreover, to be given the courage to apologize when she is wrong. She needs to be helped to find something that she can do, to go through with a job that she has begun and to make a success of it. She needs to face and to make the most of life as she finds it.

Why do you forget? A girl may forget to do the thing which she cannot do well—her geometry, for instance. Possibly she forgets the date with the boy whom she does not like. She forgets to tell her mother that the teacher said that she must work harder in order to pass in a certain subject. Forgetting may seem to be a good way to escape punishment, to cover one's mistakes, or to keep the conscience quiet. Of course some persons believe that memory is strictly a physiological function. The fact is that people usually manage to remember the things that they want to remember. The grown-up way is to face the difficult or unpleasant experiences, understand what makes them difficult, and learn from each mistake.

If the question is one of really forgetting specific matters, a girl can usually work out a method by means of which she can jog her memory. As an example, she might note the kinds of things that she forgets in her schoolwork, and hitch them to the things that she does not usually forget. If she loves English but is prone to forget her mathematics assignments because she hates mathematics, she might keep both subjects in the same notebook. She can generally tie an idea she does not like to one she does; then she will probably not forget either. She can make a logical connection between the two ideas, so that one calls up the picture of the other.

Daydreams. One way in which people may escape having to meet difficulties and to look at failures is to deny even to themselves that their limitations exist and go on blithely pretending that they are superior persons. If you adopt such a scheme of behavior, you may become the sort of person who is shocked and hurt when anyone criticizes you—you had no idea that you had any faults! Gradually a person may retire entirely into a world of her own making where she sees herself always as successful, always as the sort of person she wants to be.

An exaggerated case of daydreaming is the example of a very studious boy who lived with two maiden aunts in a poor home and saw very little of other young people. He pretended that he was a prince, that his family was very wealthy and powerful, that people hung on his words, and that every girl who met him wanted to marry him. Finally, he began almost believing these things himself. He began to tell stories about his family and about the many girls whom he had known. He said to a new friend, wistfully, "Haven't I impressed you as a person who came from a palatial home?" The tendency is as old as the story of Cinderella and as modern as jet planes.

68

Escaping reality brings small comfort and never solves a problem.
If you feel inferior, find out why and do something about it.

If you behave this way occasionally, it may be because, when your own life becomes too complicated, it is comforting to escape from it into daydreams of yourself. You may, in the daydreams, live the life that you wish that you could live in reality. "Why not do it then?" you ask. One reason is that if you retire within yourself, if you do nothing to adjust yourself to the world around you, if you take the attitude that you are better than other people, someone else will have to see that you are provided with shelter, food, and clothes. Security gained in this fashion is transitory and undependable. Moreover, you are being unfair to other people. Any girl who spends much of her time daydreaming needs to be warned that she had better come down to earth.

Of course, we all need to have *some* daydreams. The best ones are those which are possible and constructive. If you have a vivid imagination, if you can clearly picture the goals that you hope to achieve in life, you will be more likely to attain these goals in reality. However, your daydreams must be as near as possible to what is reality for you, to something that you can be and do in the future if you will work for it. In other words, translate your dreams into reality, use them to spur you on to greater accomplishments, to the honest facing of each difficulty. Do not substitute them for action. You will soon learn that you can get more fun out of real accomplishments than out of imaginary ones.

Do you need thrills? Still another way in which some girls avoid facing failure is by running around looking for thrills that will keep their minds occupied so that they do not have to think of their failures. This alone is not bad if it is confined to such activities as going to football games, riding in roller coasters or airplanes, or tobogganing. But some things you get a thrill from may endanger other people or damage property. Speeding is an example. At best, this kind of escape is a poor substitute for facing problems.

Why try to "put it over"? Cheating is a method that some girls use when they are faced with a situation in which they think they are going to fail. This applies not only to examinations but to a number of other situations. There are girls who are always trying to "put something over" on someone—their parents, their teachers, or their friends. They cannot face the possibility of failure, and they cheat or lie because they fear that they might fail if they attempted to gain their objective honestly. A girl may have begun this kind of behavior early in life—by trying to get out of doing the dishes, by taking the praise that should have gone to someone else, by copying the answers to her arithmetic assignment.

Sometimes when a girl plays truant from school, she is trying to escape from what she fears may be failure, from a situation in which she feels inadequate. Sometimes people fool themselves into thinking that drinking can give them courage. They may see themselves talking well, meeting any difficulty—but how temporary is that feeling! When you are confronted by failure, you need real courage. You cannot cheat yourself, be a coward, or run away into an imaginary world. You need to face the hard things in this real world.

"Oh, yes, you can!" A girl may think that if she parades her inferiorities, she will win sympathy. People will think that she is modest, and she will fool herself into thinking that she is quite virtuous. Consequently, she takes up people's time by telling them what mediocre work she does in certain subjects or how poor a memory she has. She begins every task with loud protestations that she "can't" do it. Such an attitude is very convenient; it makes it easy for a girl to escape doing what she does not like to do or what is difficult for her to do. It may lead people to praise her more when she does accomplish something. It is much easier than setting high standards and working to meet them.

71

The danger in the procedure is that people may take her seriously. If she continues this behavior, they may never give her a chance to do anything. Then she loses still more confidence in herself. What she needs is to have someone say to her, "Oh, yes, you can!" and then actually to find out that she can succeed at something.

"Poor me!" Some girls expend a great deal of energy in pitying themselves. They think that nobody cares about them, nobody notices them. They plan ways to make people notice them. For instance, one girl thought, "I could run away from home. Then my family would miss me and be sorry that they hadn't been nicer to me. Maybe if I had an accident, they'd all appreciate me." She had a grand time imagining her family weeping over her and wishing that they had been kinder to her.

Another method that some girls use for getting attention is to play the martyr, to glory in the fact that they are being abused. You know the kind of girl who always "gets all the dirty work," the older person who is constantly made to work overtime and to work too hard. Work alone never yet caused a breakdown, but a person's attitude toward it has.

Girls who use such methods want to have other people bolster their self-confidence, assure them that they are not as bad as they thought they were. It must be proved to such girls that only through real successes can they gain the attention that they crave.

"I don't feel well." Sometimes girls who are afraid to face difficult situations or who don't really want to assume grown-up responsibilities may use illness as a means of escaping them. People don't expect a sick girl to pass an exam or to do the housework. Instead they take care of her, give her attention, perhaps "baby" her anxiously.

In some cases, a girl is just pretending to have a headache or nausea, or to feel weak and dizzy. She is deliberately making up excuses. Other times, a girl really *is* sick. She may develop a severe headcold; she may vomit; she may even really faint. Yet this girl, too, may be using illness to avoid difficulties or to get attention, although she may not realize this. She has formed the habit of not facing her problems, and she probably learned when she was a small child that illness can be an effective excuse for not doing something or for failing in what she did attempt. Such girls need to recognize the fact that they are "running away" by becoming sick. They need to face the reasons for this behavior. That is, they need to confront their fears of failure or their feelings of inadequacy and try to overcome them.

There are similar devices to which girls may resort in order to avoid facing problems. For example, a girl may have discovered early in life that, when her mother asked her to go to the store, if she could say that she did not hear her mother call, she would not be so likely to be punished for not obeying at once. Or perhaps she found that, if she complained that her eyes hurt so much that she could not do her lessons, she was given permission to go out to a baseball game that she might otherwise have missed. It may be that she once became nervous or rigid when something frightened, worried, or excited her. She repeated this device. The next time that she wanted to avoid doing something, she developed a case of nerves, or she "just got stiff and couldn't move." Everyone around her became concerned, and she was spared. Whether such a girl realizes it or not, repeated use of these "symptoms" is an attempt either to gain attention or to avoid facing a situation that might end in failure.

On rare occasions a girl may go still further—she may

threaten suicide. It is quite true that the girl who broods too much, who thinks of herself as a failure, who sees only her own inadequacies, or the girl who, for any of a number of reasons, is very unhappy, may in all seriousness sometimes entertain thoughts of suicide. She has gotten so low in her spirits that, as one girl expressed it, "she could jump into the Grand Canyon."

However, it is well to remember that usually a girl who talks loudly and hysterically about her plans to commit suicide, who angrily threatens her household or friends by repeatedly declaring such intentions, is not really planning to carry out the threat. Though she is truly unhappy, she is merely demanding attention by her wails.

There are some cases, infrequent though they may be, of girls who have unconsciously pretended to be ill—who have, in fact, become apparently so ill that it was necessary for them to undergo an operation. After all, how can a physician know, when a girl has developed tender spots, even temperature and swelling, that she is unconsciously pretending? One quiet, unassuming girl whom no one noticed in school discovered that, when one of the other girls had an appendix operation at a hospital near school, many of the boys and girls took her flowers, stopped to see her, chatted outside the window, and when she returned to school were very thoughtful of her. A few weeks later the first girl suddenly had to have an operation for appendicitis.

None of this is said to imply that a person may not, in reality, be ill. That would be absurd. Of course, we all have experiences which prove that our emotions—our fears, our feelings of inadequacy—can affect our body functions. We all know, for instance, that one's stomach may feel queer just before an exam or just before making one's first public speech. The point is that if a girl recognizes the true causes of such symptoms, yet forms the habit of facing the difficult things that she has to do in spite of the symptoms, the symptoms generally disappear. On the other hand, if she takes advantage of any symptom of illness in order to escape doing her job or facing her problems, she may form the habit of becoming sick.

It is most unwise for a girl to use illness or threats of suicide to avoid facing the real problem. Psychologists would say that she is *rationalizing*. They would say that the girl has been making up reasons to explain her failure, instead of facing and admitting the true reasons. Instead of admitting that she failed because she did not try hard enough to succeed, because she attacked a task too difficult for her, or because of any other reason equally valid, she is pretending, to herself and to people around her that she failed because she did not feel well or because she was overworked. She considers these to be good, logical reasons, and has convinced herself that they are the correct ones because she wants to think so, or because they are the socially acceptable ones. The louder and oftener that she repeats these excuses, the more sure she becomes that they are the truth.

If she continues such a scheme of behavior until it becomes habitual, she will be throwing away one of the best chances that she has to grow up—the chance to face her problems as they are presented to her. What is more, as she retreats into this behavior, she will inevitably discover that it is most unpleasant. She misses a great deal of fun. She loses the companionship of her friends if she is too often hindered in doing things with them because she is ill. Nor will she be considered an attractive person if she is always pitying herself, if she can talk about nothing but her operation, or if she is always complaining about her aches and pains.

Most important of all, a girl's estimate of herself will rise considerably, she will find a great deal more satisfaction in life and will get more of a kick out of it, if she can take her share of responsibility in every situation she meets. When she is no longer spending her time concentrating on her own unhappiness, when she has developed confidence to face life's problems, she will wonder why she ever was so short-sighted as to choose the methods of escape described above.

"I just am this way!" You will, of course, as you go through life, sometimes find a girl who never seems to play according to the rules of the game. This is because of her past experiences; she has learned to play differently. She has been taught to get out when she was not winning, to cheat or to make a scene in an attempt to win, to avoid getting in the game when she thought that she might fail, to play as if she were the only person who counted in the game. You will find such girls because each person is today what her previous experiences have made her.

"Then," you may say, "if the kind of person I am depends upon my past experiences, there is nothing that I can do about it. I just am this kind of person." If you have read the chapter preceding this one, you know why this is not true. You know that there is much that you can do about it. You need not remain the kind of person that you are now. You will have new problems every day of your life. Hundreds of experiences will be presented to you in the coming years. Will they challenge you, or will they threaten you? You may have been afraid to face difficulties. You may not have met life in the past. Do you know now that you can meet it in the future? Your future self will be determined by the way in which you meet whatever experiences life may bring from this time on.

Runaways. One insistent tendency that some girls have to watch is the desire to run away when they have been hurt, the feeling that they cannot face people again after they have failed at something. They assume that other people expect them to fail; therefore, they cannot face difficulties again because they "just know" that they cannot meet them. They want to escape from it all. Even a desire for death may become real. We all have such feelings sometimes.

If you know that you have failed in meeting a problem, if you have lost your best friend because of your stupidity in handling the relationship, or if you have been hurt, you may become frightened; you may refuse to face the actual situation even long enough to discover why you blundered. You turn and run around the corner and hide, now and then sticking out your head fearfully to look at people or to hear what they are saying about you.

Someone may have referred to the situation and told you that you "should be ashamed" of yourself. Perhaps you become too ashamed—so ashamed that soon you forget what it was that you were to be ashamed about and you remember only that you are a low, inferior person who should be ashamed. You feel that your entire life is a failure, that you are unworthy of your friends, of having anyone care for you. You had abilities, and you failed to use them. You had friends, and you hurt them. You are always making mistakes and doing the wrong thing. Now people do not want you around. If you join them, you are only thrusting yourself on them. So your mind runs in the depths of these delusions of

77

unworthiness. When you have retreated in this fashion, it may take coaxing and a deep belief in you on the part of some understanding person to make you venture forth from your hiding place. Your own sense of inadequacy is so great that you will resist having to face again what you consider certain failure.

However, one way in which you can be helped is to be given the feeling that there is someone who will stand by, someone who cares and believes in you. But even that belief is not enough. You must be helped to move from confidence in another person's belief in you to a belief in yourself. You must learn to trust yourself more. How will you learn to do that?

Much depends upon the experiences that you have, but even more depends upon the way in which you meet them. It is your ability to go through life's difficulties, not the difficulties themselves, that gives you cause for trusting or distrusting yourself. Some girls find a way of facing difficulties as they come. Anne Frank was like this, and the girl whom we called Adrian at the beginning of the chapter. No problem ever thrusts such girls into the depths. They have a sense of confidence about meeting even their most difficult problems, because they know that they have been able to meet each lesser problem as it came. They are grown-up in their attitude toward life.

Of some girls this is not true. They do not really learn until they have been hurt enough to force them to think, until they have come to a crisis in their lives. If you are like that, you probably will not grow up until you have had a severe disappointment, until someone has hurt you terribly, until all that you thought you were and could do seems to lie in ruins, until the whole structure of your life has been threatened and you have had to give up the thing that you wanted, or thought that you wanted, most.

Some girls have this experience early in life—when the head of a family, or a loved one, dies; when the family loses its money and a girl finds, for instance, that she cannot go to college; when a friend whom she trusted lets her down; when her boy friend leaves her "flat." Anne Frank had her life uprooted when she and her family were forced into hiding; she had to give up friends, school, freedom, even air and sunshine.

She did not yield to bitterness; she learned to face her problems—and to grow up. It was anything but easy. In her diary [2] she wrote,

My head is haunted by so many wishes and thoughts, accusations and reproaches. I'm really not as conceited as so many people seem to think. I know my own faults and shortcomings better than anyone, but the difference is that I also know I want to improve, shall improve, and have already improved a good deal. . . . In addition to this, I have lots of courage, I always feel so strong and as if I can bear a great deal, I feel so free and so young! I was glad when I first realized it, because I don't think I shall easily bow down before the blows that inevitably come to everyone.

I have one outstanding trait in my character—and that is my knowledge of myself. I can watch myself and my actions, just like an outsider. The Anne of every day I can face entirely without prejudice, without making excuses for her and watch what's good and what's bad about her. . . . Every time I open my mouth, I know as soon as I've spoken whether

[2] From: *ANNE FRANK: The Diary of a Young Girl,* by Anne Frank. Copyright 1952 by Otto H. Frank. Copyright 1952 by the American Jewish Committee, reprinted by permission of Doubleday and Company, Inc.

"that ought to have been different" or "that was right as it was." There are so many things about myself that I condemn; I couldn't begin to name them all. I understand more and more how true Daddy's words were: "all children must look after their own upbringing!" Parents can only give good advice or put them on the right paths, but the final forming of a person's character lies in their own hands.

Some girls who have a bitter experience early learn from it; others do not. Instead, they run away; they do not want to be hurt. Or they thrust such an experience far back in their minds, saying that they want to forget it. Perhaps, also, adults may step in to make things easier for these girls—to comfort them, to give them what they want, possibly to protect them from the consequences of their own mistakes. Still other girls do not have such an experience until later in life. Even then, they may or may not learn from it.

The point is that when trouble comes and you are cornered, what do you do? Do you escape, excuse yourself, blame other people or fate, talk about being disillusioned, or run away? A crisis is your opportunity to prove yourself. Only when it takes every ounce of courage and self-confidence to come through, when no one else can make your decisions or fight your battles for you, only then do you find out what kind of person you really are.

You know what you can do only if you have taken the trouble to do it. You need not have any more confidence in yourself than that. Go out and succeed at something. Hiding because of fear will never be the escape that it may seem to be. It is merely solitary confinement. Nor will being ashamed really help you either. It takes your eyes off the job that you should be doing. It is necessary that you belong to the outside world. You cannot separate yourself from other people, and you have seen that, if you distrust and hurt yourself, you soon will distrust and hurt other people. Therefore, since you never hurt anyone unless you are afraid, you must not allow yourself to be frightened and beaten. You must stand ready for life. Begin doing something at which you have a fair chance of success. The experience of success, together with the praise it brings, will give you more courage to try again. You will no longer need to run away.

It is to be expected, naturally, that some difficulties, some bitter experiences, may get you down temporarily. But if you have grown up, they cannot *keep* you down. You recognize the things that you can do well. You do them and work on others that you need to improve. You do not feel inferior because there are some things that you cannot do. You have gained confidence in yourself. You have a belief in life. You have the ability to face life. You have a method to use in facing it. And so you bounce back, after hurts and disillusionments, ready to begin again.

Living With Uncertainty

Everyone wakes each morning to problems to which he or she must seek solutions. Since no two real-life problems are ever alike, no ready-made solutions exist; one must think one's way out of each situation—and one cannot always be right!

How does one learn to live with this uncertainty? Some girls see only danger in each new day. Some pretend not to see, hoping that what they fear will go away if they don't notice it. Others are haunted by fears! Like children listening for spooks tapping on their bedroom windows, they allow the terrors of former mistakes to hover over them. They expect the worst of themselves. Such a girl might say that she "is too smart to hope for anything ever again." She'd rather be wrong and "have it over with" than take a chance that she is right but live with uncertainty while she waits to find out.

Another girl's philosophy may be: "The way out is the way through. When I have something to decide, I want to get it over with, so I plough through as fast as I can." She asks no favors, only opportunity to show what she can do. She makes mistakes, but they never shackle her initiative. She is justly proud of her independence of mind and behavior. She may act before she thinks, but at least she grapples with her problems as they appear; she sweats it out rather than sitting it out!

More realistic, however, than the girl who is fearful or the one who is impulsive is the one who calmly sizes up each new situation. When she finds herself facing a problem about which she does not know enough, she *deliberately* postpones action. She chooses to live with uncertainty while she initiates a problem-solving approach. She seeks information and gathers clues to form a basis for responsible future action.

Over the wide range of human problems, there are no easy answers. If a girl is eventually to make wise decisions, she must learn to look again, seek more facts, listen to more people, weigh more alternatives. It is a process that demands time and skill; it might be described as "watchful waiting." However, deliberately to postpone action when the pressure to *do something* is great is, in itself, a difficult action. Girls differ in their tolerance of this watchful waiting; some even misunderstand it as procrastination. A mature girl recognizes it as the process by which she gives herself a chance at success and minimizes the possibility of failure. This girl has learned to live with uncertainty.

CHAPTER FOUR

Growing Up Emotionally

IN EARLIER chapters some of the factors involved in growth toward emotional maturity have been described. Emphasis has been placed on the fact that to be a well-adjusted adult a person must be grown-up in her handling of the emotions of fear and anger. Standards of emotional maturity were set up, standards such as these: The mature person is seldom angry, but when she is, there is just cause for her anger. The mature person knows her limitations and does not continually defend herself against or blame others for her failures or mistakes. The mature person confronts whatever she fears in a situation and learns how to handle her fears.

There is a third emotion, that of love, which you must learn to view as an adult. The measure of your emotional maturity in your conception of love is: How far have you progressed from the place where your only interest is in yourself toward the place where you care deeply about other people? It was also observed earlier that it is quite possible for a girl to be grown-up in her handling of some of her emotions and quite immature in regard to others. For instance, she may be comparatively honest with herself in her consideration of the extent and kind of ability which she possesses, yet not be able to control infantile temper tantrums. Various other types of behavior were discussed at length in Chapter 3 and labeled *infantile*.

In the course of a girl's growth toward a mature conception of love, it is necessary, as in other growth, to pass through various levels of development. Some girls move along smoothly in making these adjustments. They seem to be progressing relatively easily toward emotional maturity. Other girls are blocked at various levels of development. Some girls never move from the infantile level. A girl who habitually uses immature behavior and who habitually shows a lack of emotional maturity in her conception of love is described as being *self-centered*.

Your Self

What are some of the stages of development that might be considered characteristic of some individuals in any group of high school girls? There is the "show-off" stage. You have seen the kind of girl who apparently knows no other way of attracting attention to herself than by wearing extreme clothes, using too much make-up—or none at all, showing off the latest steps in dancing. She is interested in no one but herself. She seems to spend all her time devising ways in which to assert herself. This self-centered stage of emotional development is called the *narcissistic* stage, from the myth about the Greek youth named Narcissus who saw his own image in the water and fell in love with it.

It is natural for a baby to be self-centered, for normally everyone is, at first, most interested in herself and in her own comfort. Bend over a tiny baby's crib, and watch her. She scarcely knows where the blankets end and where she

84

The right amount of make-up, carefully applied, is important in good grooming.

begins. She acts as though she were absorbed in discovering that those objects waving above her, her hands and feet, belong to herself. She seems to be attempting to prove to herself that they are hers by putting them in her mouth. Her love and affection are centered primarily on herself. She must have all the attention. She demands instant relief from any discomfort. When she is hungry or uncomfortable or forced to do anything which she does not like, she cries. Her cries become loud protests when she does not get what she wants immediately. She does not know what it means to wait for something that she wants or to be considerate of other people's wants.

The self-centered girl has not yet completely grown out of this stage. It was natural for her to act in these ways as a baby, but if she still resorts to such behavior, she is regressing, going back to acting like a baby. When she was a baby, it was also natural for her to show off. She may, in childhood, have been encouraged too strenuously to do so. Or she may have been discouraged, even punished, when she attempted to show off. However, there is no excuse for her spending the rest of her life showing off. She needs to discard these infantile ways of attracting attention and to learn others which will be more acceptable with people of her own age.

This period of infancy is the normal one for a baby to discover her own body. As the baby explores all of this body which belongs to her—as she finds her hands, her feet, her face—she discovers her genital organs, too, just as she does other parts of her body. If adults do not frighten her or slap her or shame her, if they look upon this exploration of her body as a natural occurrence and do not worry about it, the baby soon turns to other things. Her interest passes to a toy or to something else new. Most children thus grow naturally away from self-interest to an interest in the world outside themselves. This growth continues as they grow older; they find other and more interesting activities with which to occupy their time.

However, girls, from about twelve to sixteen years of age pass through another stage when they pay a great deal of attention to themselves. If, by the time girls are in high school, they have not become absorbed in sports, dramatics, or other creative activities, if they do not seem to get along with other girls and boys, if they have not had an opportunity to have companionable good times with their boy and girl friends and they feel that nobody likes them, then they may return to their childish habits of self-interest, self-love, and self-stimulation. They may do so because they are lonely or because they feel inadequate. Nevertheless, when they resort to such behavior, they sometimes have such a sense of guilt or fear or shame about it that they feel still more inferior. If a girl worries about it or has developed feelings of sin or guilt about her behavior, she may become badly adjusted emotionally.

As far as doctors can tell, such a habit, in itself, does not cause any physical diseases. Nor have they found any evidence that the practice causes insanity. Actually, it is a way of slipping back to childhood and being exclusively concerned with oneself. As such, it leads to nothing of value and is a sign of emotional immaturity.

It is more satisfying and more sensible for high school girls to put their energies into learning how to be good friends to both boys and girls, into being gracious and attractive and having a good time socially, into developing skill in some sport, or into finding a deep interest in some art or hobby. These activities will give them valuable experience, carry them out of themselves, help them to become interesting persons, and bring them the love and friendship that they desire.

Parents

The first step from the stage in which a child tries only to satisfy her own desires, regardless of the effect on other people or on herself, comes when—because of her need for love and security—she is able to consider the desires of her parents. Early in a baby's life, she is able to distinguish certain people from all that goes on around her. Usually the first person of whom she becomes conscious or whom she "loves" is her mother, because her mother is the one who does things for her. Her mother feeds her, keeps her com-

87

fortable, amuses her, and comforts her when she is in pain. The baby seems to know that her mother is necessary to her, that she is, indeed, the most important part of her environment. Therefore, the baby begins alternately to scheme to keep her mother near her and to fear that she will leave her. The baby regulates her behavior accordingly. She watches her mother; she does things that will please her mother in order to have attention drawn to herself and continue to have things done for her.

Soon the baby finds that there is someone else in the picture—her father. She discovers that he, too, can give her things or deprive her of them. These two people seem omnipotent. The baby is helpless; consequently, she learns to do whatever is necessary to remain in her parents' good graces and to remain secure. This is particularly difficult for the child if her father and mother are not happy together, if they cannot agree on the way to treat the child, or if they become rivals for her affections. Then a child feels nervous, unhappy, insecure, and may tend to be fearful for the rest of her life.

On the other hand, the child may be so happy at this stage, she may find it so easy and so comfortable to be taken care of, and her parents may so enjoy doing it that she never grows any farther emotionally. You know the kind of girl who cannot make her own decisions: She has to be told what dress to wear; she cannot begin doing anything without running to her parents for reassurance; she cannot go away from home, because she always becomes homesick. If a girl continues to live in this sheltered state—being taken care of, having all her wants satisfied, never having to do anything for herself—she will remain emotionally on a childish level, unprepared for a mature experience of love. She knows only how to take; she has never learned to give.

Childhood Playmates

People other than parents should become a part of the child's life early. These people may be her older brothers and sisters—or even a new baby, of whom the child may be jealous at first, because the baby takes some of her parents' time which the child thinks belongs to her. Having brothers and sisters creates some problems; nevertheless, it is very important for every child to know other children. When she has brothers, sisters, and playmates, she *has* to begin to learn how to get along with them. Most of them are infantile and selfish in their behavior, just as she is. They may boss her, tease her, make fun of her. She may run home to tell Mother; she may find a place to play by herself; or she may, perhaps, be the strongest, and manage to lord it over the other children.

On the other hand, she may learn that it is more fun to share her toys with other people. They like her then and allow her to play with their toys. Possibly she may learn that, if she plays somebody else's game this time, the group will play her game next. A child's feeling of success at this period comes not only from the things that she and her playmates do together—the games that they play, the houses that they build—but also from the degree to which she feels herself one of the group. She must know that the other children accept and like her.

Every girl needs to have this experience of playing with children of her own age. If she does not, she may stand still, be blocked emotionally at this stage. Later, she may become the coquettish woman who thinks that she is being "cute" when she suggests that "we'll all be girls together," or the playful middle-aged matron who is always planning practical jokes. She may have been the wistful fat girl on whom the jokes were played. Each of these women is still trying to impress her crowd. In other words, a girl's first play experiences may give her confidence and security, overconfidence and a false sense of security, or insecurity and an actual fear or people. This last possibility may require a hard fight if she is to conquer it later in life. The attitudes created in a girl because of the way in which she did or did not manage to get along with her playmates in her childhood may help to explain why it is easy or difficult for her to get along with people now.

Best Friends

At first a child is no more conscious of the distinction between sexes among her playmates than adults force her to be—that is, if she is fortunate enough to have both boys and girls to play with. However, as a girl enters her teens, she becomes interested in people as individuals. She differentiates between the sexes, and she begins to look for special friends. These special friends are, at first, probably girls. A girl is not quite ready for boys as close friends. She prefers someone like herself. Every girl wants to be popular with many people, but at this stage a girl may want also to have a best friend, a girl friend with whom she can share intimate confidences. To have a friend is worth a great deal more than any amount of general popularity. A girl needs someone outside of her family with whom she can feel absolutely comfortable. She gains security and belief in herself through the knowledge that this other person considers her worthy of friendship.

Sometimes, however, this friendship becomes an all-absorbing interest. Then girls call it a "crush." You all know what a crush is like. A girl wants always to be with her friend. She spends most of her time in this one girl's presence, even though she may sometimes feel that she is not particularly welcome. She may protest whenever the girl goes out with anyone else. She may have fits of the blues and cry when she thinks that the girl has neglected her. In general, she may make life miserable for herself and for her friend.

Behavior of this kind indicates that a girl is taking another one of the natural steps in the long process of growing up emotionally. The girl in her teens is in the process of being weaned away from her family toward her own independence, but because she cannot yet stand alone, she is clinging for a little while to someone else. The danger in this tendency is that a girl may expend all her emotional energy on another girl because she does not know how to meet boys, has not had an opportunity to meet them, or is afraid of them. Then such behavior becomes a serious problem, because she may stop growing up at this stage. She needs, next, to be weaned away from a too absorbing interest in another girl or in a woman and encouraged to take another step—to learn to know boys.

A girl often feels a great admiration for adults who, in her estimation, are "in." These adults are the kinds of people whom she wants to be like some day; they are doing the kinds of things that she pictures herself as doing. They personify her ideals. She would like a personality, a hair-do, a figure, manners, or clothes like someone whom she admires. She would like to play the piano so well that she would stir the same emotions that she feels when the "wonderful man" heading the music department plays. She would like to be as chic and as successful as the dress buyer in the department store where she works.

The people whom the girl idealizes may be individuals whom she knows or even ones whom she has met only in books, on the screen, or in plays. They may be teachers or family friends, movie or television stars, the popular girls in high school, or the girls who have special talents. A girl, in the process of growing up, usually sees one person after another whom she admires for a long or short time. This practice helps a girl to see more clearly what she hopes some day to become. Your emotions are the drive for your ambition. You pattern your actions after those of people who fire your ambition. One person's influence lasts with you as long as the person typifies some part of this ambition.

If a girl can make friends with these people, she may want to spend all her time with them. She may become jealous if they notice someone else. She will agree with all that they say; she will flatter them; she may give them gifts. If she cannot become well acquainted with these people, she may worship them from afar, continually quote their opinions to her family and friends, imitate their clothes or their manners, write poetry to them, or sleep with their pictures under her pillow.

Such relationships with adults can help in the process of growing up. When a girl is uncertain of herself, she is helped immensely by encouragement in her ambitions or by genuine consideration for her welfare given by an adult whom she admires. But when a girl finds that a mature woman seems to be reciprocating the intensity of her feelings, to be developing a crush on her, she needs to be wary. When adults are admired in this way, some may be unwise enough to take the adoration seriously. They may feel personally flattered, or they may gain satisfaction for their own need for admiration and love through a girl's attentions.

It will help a girl in such a situation if she will realize that it is not this particular person in whom she is really interested; it is this person's achievements and abilities that she admires and desires to have. Or, if a girl has not yet learned how to make her own decisions or how to do things for herself, she may be looking for a second mother. If her mother is not demonstrative and affectionate enough to make her feel that she is loved deeply, she may try to find someone else who will love her. Everyone needs such love and the feeling of security which it brings. It is difficult to grow out of one stage until a girl has had all the satisfactions from it that she should have had.

A real danger in such an intense emotional attachment is that a girl may draw weakness instead of strength from this relationship. She may be kept from gaining self-confidence. Her special friend may become a mother-substitute. A girl may become too dependent on her friend; without that friend she cannot make any decisions, she cannot stand on her own feet, and all that she does is done with an eye to gaining her friend's attention and approval. In other words, when she finds a person in whose friendship she feels security, she may lose her personality completely in that person in order to keep her security. Her friend may absorb all of her affection. She may idolize this friend so blatantly that the friend may even resent and be embarrassed by her idolatry and indecision. She is taking out her emotions on her friend possibly because she is too lazy or frightened to proceed to the next level of emotional development. The friend probably would prefer a more mature relationship in which neither personality is subordinated to the other.

On the other hand, some of the most precious and lasting friendships of girls' lives may begin at this age. The girls whom you like very much, the older persons whom you admire, can help you a great deal in this period of your adjustment if you both are wise in the kind of relationship that you work out together. If you use love in a mature fashion, you find that your own feelings can help you to understand—and feel *with*—other people. Deeply caring for other people can make life full and interesting for you. Breadth and sincerity of feelings means richness in living.

Do not fear your emotions. Do not be afraid to care deeply for other people and to let them know that you admire and like them. Some girls have so repressed their feelings that they have sometimes hurt their friends by their inability to show love and appreciation. Other girls have hesitated to express their emotions, since the only expression of emotion they have known has been in an objectionable form such as raging or nagging. These fearful people have never *learned* how to express positive emotions in words or gestures of affection. Therefore, they are unsure of themselves, hesitant or embarrassed about expressing deep feelings of consideration, appreciation, admiration, or love.

They may, also, be afraid to tell a friend how much they care for her because that person then has the power to hurt them. They may have been hurt in the past; they do not want to be hurt again. Those whom we love are the only people in this world who really have the power to hurt us. However, a person who cannot trust someone else sufficiently to place herself in that person's hands, knowing that she may be hurt, can never know mature love, because fear destroys love.

There is also the girl who makes the development of a genuine friendship impossible for herself because she is afraid that her friend will not like her if her friend finds out what sort of person she really is. This girl feels inadequate. She may brood or blame herself because her experiences and accomplishments are different and not so varied as those of her friend. This lack of belief in herself haunts her. She may have been scolded about her inadequacies at some time in the past; she may have been frightened into the opinion that she has nothing to give. Consequently, she flies to her friend when she is afraid to face the world alone; she depends on her friend to protect her from the results of her own mistakes. She takes out on her friend her despair of herself. She consumes a great deal of the time which they spend together by a recital of her own limitations and weaknesses. Such behavior is cruelty to herself and to her friend. Not only is she preying on her friend's emotions, but also she is reinforcing her own feeling of inadequacy by continuing to think that she has nothing to give in their relationship.

You should, by all means, have a good friend, but you should not stand on your friend's feet. A girl who does so is lazy and cowardly. You need, instead, to depend on yourself. This you will learn to do by facing whatever life brings, not by sitting down on the job or by attempting to escape the difficult things. You need to gather resources that will build up your security. You must take every opportunity presented you to know many people. As you learn to enjoy a variety of people, you will no longer wish to spend all your time and emotion on one person. If you are interested in nothing save one individual's likes and dislikes, how can others be interested in you?

Therefore, dive into life! True, you may hit flat at first, but you'll be a person, not a poor copy of someone else. You will learn, from the experiences that daily present themselves, to do many things for yourself and by yourself. This leaves you free to be at your best when you are with your friend. Then you will be sensitive to *her* needs, not conscious only of your own. You will become an understanding person, one who can use your emotions to feel *with* another person.

Of course your experiences and your accomplishments will be different from your friend's. No one person can have all the enviable accomplishments and be everything; we all can be something. We are all at different stages in this process of growing up. It is up to us to encourage each other. Mature friendship must be on the basis of complete trust and respect for one another as two different persons who understand each other and who care a great deal about each other. You expect to talk over your difficulties with your friend. You do not shut yourself off entirely, refusing to let anyone get at you because you are afraid of your limitations; you are not on the defensive about them. It is no longer necessary to seek to excuse yourself, because you know that your friend understands all about you—and likes you—just as you are!

Such help must be mutual. A real friendship must be based on understanding, not on one person's domination of the other, or on one's patronizing the other. Though your friend may have acquired a considerable influence over you, your feelings and opinions are also respected by her.

If you can work out this kind of relationship with a friend, then you need never quarrel with her, be jealous of her, or be unhappy because you are not like her. You recognize in your differences the contribution that you have to make to each other. You are always ready to share your experience when your friend needs you or asks your help. You each give your best to the other, yet you do not absorb each other. You both remain free to learn what you can from life, each in your own way, and to make your contribution to other people. In the future, you will look back upon this experience of genuine friendship and find that it has given you deep joy. It will have been a help, not a hindrance, in growing up, because you have learned, by means of it, to care unselfishly for someone else in the world.

Widening Your Relationships

The basis for understanding the level of your own emotional maturity is to know what the whole range of maturing is and then to recognize and to face particular behavior as it appears. Do not just drift. You must know when you are running back to the protection of childhood. Watch yourself. Recognize what is happening when you are overprotected and overindulged at any stage in ways that make you content to stay at that stage when you should be growing out of it.

Ask yourself honestly whether you are self-centered. Are you still expending all your energy in admiration of, or concern over, yourself? Do you enjoy the protection that it gives you to have your mother do everything for you? Are you pouring out all your emotion on one special friend with whom you feel secure? Are you afraid of boys because there are no boys in your family? If your first knowledge of sex came in a way that frightened or disgusted you, have you had an opportunity to learn that most people think of sex as a natural and beautiful part of life? Any of these circumstances may block you at one of the childish levels unless you make an effort to deal with the difficulty as intelligently as possible.

Make friends with boys and girls who have many different interests and abilities.

Your aim now must be to know many people and to include boys among your friends. A wise girl friend or older friend will be able to recognize this fact and can help you to make the transition to good times which include boys. Such a friend might help by inviting you to a party and standing by to see that you have a good time, by taking you out on "double dates," or by helping you to make yourself more attractive.

You need to learn to know boys in order that, in time, you

may become independent of your family and care enough for someone else to set up a home of your own, to have children yourself, and, finally, to gain your happiness by giving it to others in your home and in your community. When you can see your life as an opportunity to do things for others, and you can graciously accept things done for you, then you are grown-up emotionally.

Learning about Love

When you hear the word "love," what do you think of? Perhaps you think of "falling in love" as though love were something into which you were unwillingly precipitated, like falling into a lake! For many girls, the word means only a personal emotion.

Today, you and a boy are "in love." You are absorbed in one another. But there is more to love than being "in love." To love means to give to someone else and to receive from someone else. Most high school girls are not yet certain of what they have to give nor of what they want to receive. You are constantly changing in your expectations of yourself and of others. Have you ever tried, when you were all alone, to find out what you want from yourself and from other people?

While you are in the midst of change, you cannot expect yourself to be steadfast, constant, and true to another human being, even if you want to be. Ten years from now, you will not be the same person you are today; you will be transformed from a girl to a woman.

Just as bodies and faces change in ten years, so also minds and emotions grow. Reason and experience will play a part in your estimate of "love" then, so you may fall out of love as you once fell in. You may consider being "in love" just a romantic dream because, by that time, you will have developed a mature concept of love; that is, you will know that there is an enormous range of meaning in this one word.

Love is a powerful emotion. In it are combined generosity and warmth, humility and pride, concern for others and concern for self, self-assertion and self-surrender.

Love is all-pervasive. No one can live without it. It includes parents' love for children; children's love for parents; brothers' and sisters' love for one another; self-love; love for one's friends, one's home, one's country, and one's ideals. It even includes love of money and power.

Love is an enlargement of life. Without parental love, children's growth would be stunted. Without personal love, the human species would die out, the individual fail to develop his potential. Without concern for others, violence and disillusion would be rampant. Without love of beauty in all its forms, the human personality would develop no sense of reverence. Love leads all life to greater fulfillment; it counteracts hate and destructive impulses with tenderness and sensitivity and understanding.

When you know who you are, what you have to give life, what you want from life, then you are ready for the joy and heartbreak of mature love like this.

So give independence a try. Give the world a try—explore it, take risks, make mistakes and learn all manner of things about yourself and other people. In the process, you will experience love in many forms.

CHAPTER FIVE

Getting Along with People

As you read the last chapter, it probably became increasingly clear to you that you can be conscious of your "self" only in relation to other people. You measure whatever you do or fail to do in relation to the achievements of others. Your character, your criteria of what is worthwhile in life, your ideal of the kind of person that you want to be—all these come through what you learn from your experiences with other people. These ideas are not imposed on you. Character is not a bundle of traits with which you were born or which you were taught in school. Character develops, not with a spirit of sacrifice of your self, but, rather, with a maturity that teaches you that no self-confidence or freedom can come if you separate yourself from others.

People were made to belong to each other. No one individual can live alone. You are blind to this basic consideration if you say that your friends are uninteresting, boys are pests, or adults bore you. You cannot develop self-confidence or become a happy, well-adjusted person without understanding and learning from an ever-widening group of people. Therefore, you develop, as you truly grow up, increasing acceptance and appreciation of the worth of other people, as well as respect for your own individuality.

Why People Like You

Do you know how to get along happily with other people? Some girls neither attract nor repel people; they just fail to secure attention. That, as you know, is tragic for a girl. Of course you need to have people like you, yet have you ever inquired of yourself why they should like you? Some girls unthinkingly expect people to like them for no other reason than that they are pretty, that they are smart, that they wear their clothes well, or that they have money to spend. Other girls think that they can force their teachers, for instance, to like them if they study harder than other girls or if they are more obedient in school. Sometimes, when they fail to secure the friendship of girls in school with whom they would like to be friends, they gather around themselves a few girls who will "appreciate" them, girls who will sit and worship them. They may even rationalize their failure to be accepted by the girls with whom they wish to be friends by saying that those girls are jealous of their skill in getting along with teachers.

These girls would be far wiser if they set out to discover why some people like them and then attempted in an intelligent fashion to get along with more people. The ability to get along with people does not just happen; it must be developed. Naturally, it is true that people will like you when you are the kind of person who makes them feel happy and comfortable. Your mother feels happy and comfortable when you obey her. Your teacher feels happy and comfortable when you study, because she can point you out as an example of an industrious student, a credit to her. However, if you are "too perfect," you may make your brothers and sisters or your classmates dislike you because your behavior makes them feel inferior to you, and people dislike being made to feel uncomfortable and inferior. Therefore, this matter of getting along with people often presents difficult problems, but it can be more fun than anything else in life.

Fear of people disappears as your experience with people widens. As you accumulate knowledge about people, you gradually acquire more and more confidence in dealing with them. If you really make an effort to understand people, they will generally like you, and your increased understanding of them will probably mean that you gain in appreciation of them. Thus, in the process of trying to understand people, you acquire a method of dealing with them. You gain courage from this knowledge that you *can* build up satisfactory relationships with people. Thus you increase your poise and self-confidence.

Each new relationship in your ever-widening circle involves ability to identify yourself with the interests and needs of some other individual. How soon you acquire this ability depends upon your insight into the reasons why people need one another. What every person hopes for from another is security, response, recognition, and new experience. Psychologists call these *fundamental needs of personality*.

Everyone needs to feel happy, comfortable, wanted, and secure in her knowledge that she is worthwhile because someone else cares about her. Therefore, your liking for a person must be a genuine one if your relationship is to be meaningful. You must honestly want to understand people and to believe in them. This will help them to acquire confidence to be their best selves. At the same time they, in turn, will like you because your belief in them has helped them to acquire this confidence.

A girl wants also to feel that someone else is responding to her proposal of friendship. Everyone needs the confidence which comes from knowing that the best she has to offer in abilities, interests, and accomplishments is respected and appreciated. She, in turn, must be willing to recognize other people's qualities and achievements, to learn from them, and to give them credit for whatever they have to offer. Through such give-and-take in friendship, a girl enriches her own life. As people share interests, each contributes new experiences to the other. The girls who have many interests, abilities, and accomplishments to share with other people are usually those who get along well with people.

People like to be liked. You must, then, really like people. Nothing that you do can make another person respond unless you are sincere in your regard for the person. Ask yourself what conception you have of the part you wish other people to play in your life. Some girls heedlessly behave as if they thought of other people as necessary evils to be tolerated, as inferior beings to be taken advantage of—marionettes whose strings are to be pulled in order to get them to do what they want—or as superior beings to be feared and suspected lest they take advantage of them. Both these conceptions are childish and dangerous.

No individual friend is perfect—nor are you—but each can contribute something to your life. Each person will and must change as she grows up and tries out now one line of behavior, now another. Each girl must also grant to her friends this right to grow and to change. She cannot hope to dictate the way in which another person will grow and change, nor can she tolerate dictation of her own growth.

A girl, therefore, shows a great deal of intelligence when she works out for herself a conception of the part that she wishes other people to play in her life by saying to herself: "This is a large world. I want to know as much about it as possible. I cannot learn everything from books; neither can I have all the experiences myself. However, I can learn from people if I will take advantage of all my opportunities for meeting people. I will make friends with many, learning to know and appreciate people different from me—different in religion, in interests, in age, in culture, in nationality, in social and economic status. If I know nothing about music, art, poetry, literature, nature, mechanics, sports, I will not therefore shut these things out of my life. I will have friends who are particularly interested in these things. They will help me. In our companionship, they will share with me their enthusiasm. I will develop an appreciation for those things which interest them.

"I will not be afraid to make friends with a girl because of the neighborhood she lives in, because of the kind of work her father does, or because her religion or nationality are different from mine. I will set myself to know girls from many different social groups. I will find out what interests them, how they spend their time, what they think about, what they consider important in life.

"I will have among my friends some people older than I, whose ideals I appreciate, whose personalities I admire, whose advice I seek. Among my friends, I will have adults who seem to me to be superior people who have achieved success in their chosen work. Their success will give me something for which to strive. I will try to find out what contributed to their success.

"I will realize, too, that there are some adults who never achieve emotional maturity or economic security. I will learn something of their struggles. I will appreciate their difficulties. I will, therefore, be patient with, instead of annoyed by, their behavior when I see them frightened, subservient, lacking ambition, and resigned to failure, or when I see them domineering, overambitious or grasping, exploiting others, disparaging or being jealous of others, or moralizing to cover their feelings of inadequacy."

If you can develop this kind of interest in everyone, you will gain not only objectivity, or the realization that the world is much more interesting than you are, but—even more important—you will gain a sensitivity to others which is the basis of all genuine understanding. When you achieve these goals, it will be impossible for you to label people "queer" simply because they are different from you. You will realize, instead, that you resort to prejudices to cover up your own ignorance. You will admit that you are missing a great deal in life by clinging to your prejudices without questioning them—that you are prejudiced against people and things of which you know nothing. In other words, you are being "down on what you aren't up on."

People like you to go halfway. Another way of answering the question "How do you get people to like you?" is: Go halfway, at least, in developing your friendships. Begin by going halfway to get acquainted.

Do you know the story of the unhappy girl and the talisman? A high school girl was lonely and unhappy because she had no friends and did not know how to get her classmates to like her. In class she seldom talked to anyone; in the lunchroom she sat alone; after school she went home immediately. One day, when she felt that she could not bear her unhappiness any longer, she went to see an old lady, a very dear friend of hers, and told her of her loneliness. The old lady got up, unlocked a dresser drawer, and from a lovely old jewel box gave the girl a round gold medal, saying, "Here, take this and wear it tomorrow, hidden on a chain around your neck where no one can see it. It is a talisman. It will bring you friends. But it works only if you will talk first to the first five girls whom you meet in the morning." The girl doubted whether she could. What would she say? They talked about that for a while. Then the girl promised that she would fulfill her part of the compact.

She went eagerly to school the next day. The talisman seemed to work. The first girl to whom she spoke was in her first class, she discovered, and they walked to class together. The next girl asked her to join her and two others at lunch. They talked, and before she knew it, she had promised to join the school club about which they were so enthusiastic. Another girl to whom she had talked came to sit with her in the library. She rushed home, eager to leave her books and dash out to tell the old lady what a miracle the talisman had performed. As she entered her own bedroom, the first thing that she saw was the talisman, lying on the bed where it must have dropped in the morning.

This girl's experience can teach you many things. The most important is that no one can help a girl more than she wants to be helped. The best pilot in the world cannot guide a boat that is anchored. So it is with you. If you are not willing to do something for yourself, another person's efforts to help you are in vain. If you withdraw from people, become inaccessible to them, will not do your part in a relationship, if you continue to live in a past in which you are frightened and ashamed of failures instead of using your failures to teach you something that you can apply to the present, then no one can help you. If you take out your despair of yourself on other people, they will consider you tiresome and will leave you alone. People generally do not realize the truth of a statement made by Karl Menninger, a well-known psychiatrist: "The unhappy are always wrong."

Examine all your relationships with people critically. Ask yourself honestly whether you actually do go halfway in your response to people. Or are you so self-conscious, for instance, so ill at ease because you are thinking only of yourself, wondering what impression you are creating, that you make everyone around you uncomfortable? Do you shrink from making acquaintances because you are afraid of being hurt at what people may think and say about you, or do you try to learn from criticism? Can you take a "razzing," or do you become angry because it makes you feel inferior and so crushed that you are unable to make a comeback? When you fail to learn from your mistakes, do you look to yourself instead of to others for the cause of your failure?

All girls need friendship and need recognition, but some find it difficult to secure either one, because they are resorting in their relationships to second-rate forms of behavior. They have not learned better ways. Ask yourself when and why you please or irritate people. When you are with other people, do you talk about yourself and strut your good qualities, or do you go to the other extreme and sit around feeling depressed and sorry for yourself? Do you count the favors that you do for people and expect to hold

108

their friendship because of the favors? Do you bewail people's ingratitude when you find that friendship is not to be bought in this way? If you are such a person, you become like parents who repeatedly tell a girl about all the sacrifices they have made for her. This is one way of dominating a girl, and of telling her that they expect something in return for what they have given. Do you give *your* gifts in order to control others or, perhaps, to make yourself feel noble?

Have you learned to take as well as to give? You need to learn to receive favors graciously. If you remember how much satisfaction it gives you when you can give someone something that is appreciated, you will not be selfish; you will allow your friends to have the satisfaction of giving to you. Be careful, however, not to take people, their favors, and their kindness for granted. Always express your appreciation of what people do for you.

People like to be thought interesting. The next discovery to be made from the experience of the girl with the talisman is that, if you want people to like you, you must be willing to learn from them. You will find that the wider your variety of friends, the more points of view about life and living that they represent, the more you can learn from them. You can learn from girls whom you do not like, from the popular girl, from the studious girl, from the girl of another nationality, race, or religion, from older people. They all can teach you something and thereby make you a more interesting person.

There is a real place for wise adults in your life. You know from experience that you often seek eagerly the help of understanding adults. You find that you need them to point the way out of difficulties. You need them to "hang on to" until you can gain enough confidence in yourself to go forward alone. You need them to listen to, because you learn from

109

their experiences. Then you do not have to make the same mistakes that they have made. If each generation had to start out on its own and could learn nothing from the experiences of others or from the cultural heritage, progress would be slow indeed!

Of course, the adult who means most to you is not the one who only maintains his or her authority over you, who only imposes his or her will on you. It is the person who stands with you, who makes it possible for you to have experiences and responsibilities which help you to find yourself, to try out your potentialities. Such an adult keeps, always, a deep, unceasing belief in you, and in your inherent possibilities. He or she uses imagination much as a weaver who can visualize a completed pattern. The weaver works out the colors of his design in accordance with his vision of what the result will be. In the same way, adults can see, like the weaver, what the effect on your life pattern may be of each line of action that you choose. Yet they do not impose a course of action upon you. They allow you to choose because they believe in you and because they have a vision of what you can make of your life.

Such adults never desert you when you fail. They share with you what they have learned out of similar experiences. They help you to see why you have failed, help you not to be too disappointed in yourself, not to run away from difficulties. They show you how to start over again. They stand by while you try, so that through repeated experiences of success you may come to recognize your abilities, know what you can do, and be able to hold up your head because you are sure of yourself. Soon you no longer need to cling to them or to anyone. You have gained self-confidence.

Talking things over with teachers or other adults whom you admire will help you grow up.

You may object that there are not enough adults who are willing to work out such a relationship with you or who are wise enough to do so. No adult can do it alone. Wise adults genuinely interested in girls do not thrust themselves upon girls, even if they feel that girls need help. They realize the uselessness of offering help until a girl is ready for it and attests to such readiness by seeking it. In addition, they have so much respect for the integrity of a girl's personality that they will not step in and make her decisions for her. They feel that she has a right to noninterference in her life, even though she may make mistakes; therefore, they wait for an invitation from the girl. Do you ever issue that invitation? Do you seek the help available to you? Do you do your part in making it possible for adults to work with you?

People like to be understood and believed in. Last, you can learn from the girl's experience with the talisman that your own emotions, your doubts of yourself, your fear that people will not like you, your dread that you are not so good as other girls, are valuable to you. The struggles that you have in the process of growing up need not make you feel inferior. They are not burdens to be borne to make life miserable. Rather, they are lessons to be learned to help you grow up. Such struggles are your means for understanding other people, for helping them in their difficulties and struggles. Because of your own struggles, you can sense another person's need and think of that instead of holding yourself back because you think only of your own inferiority.

If you had never had any problems to face, you would have become a shallow, thoughtless person. But if you have faced your own fears and dreads and learned from them, you can apply what you have learned. You find that you are no longer willing either to blame or to snub girls because they defend and excuse themselves and their mistakes. You understand such fears and struggles. You do not become bored with immature, unattractive people; you are constructively critical of them. Because *you* have felt that way, you can be sympathetic with the people who have similar feelings of loneliness and inferiority. Most people have such feelings at some time, and it is then that they desperately need a real friend.

In every new relationship, you keep your eyes open. You never want to become so adaptable that, should you land in

112

a mud puddle, you would stay there. By all means, learn to "feel with" other people, to see things as they see them, but learn also to see people for what they are, with their limitations and their weaknesses, as well as their abilities and strengths.

Do not expect perfection of your friends. Remember that, after all, no one really knows what perfection is. We each seek a different perfection, but we each realize that we are not achieving it, and therefore we seek in others what we wish that we could find in ourselves. It is a more mature attitude neither to judge nor to idealize people but to recognize that every person has limitations and will make mistakes. Any girl who expects perfection and cannot forgive another's mistakes breaks the bridge over which she herself must pass, for we all need to be forgiven.

When these attitudes have become a part of you, you have developed the ability to see other people's points of view. You have a conviction about the importance and the worth of people which shows in all your relationships with them. You are willing to do your part in helping each individual you meet toward his or her own fullest development— toward realization of his or her own possibilities.

You have the deepest respect for, and confidence in, other people. This belief of yours helps them to be *their own* best selves, to be free, to find that "self" of theirs through their own difficulties, guided by whatever values they consider of greatest importance. You have learned that helping people to develop does not mean making them over into people like you.

How can you show genuine concern about people whom you meet? You can begin, in each new relationship, by learn-

113

ing about this new person—his or her likes, dislikes, interests, ambitions, plans for the future, ideals. You do not talk only of yourself; you listen to other people and enjoy them. You are not thinking only of the impression you are making. Nor are you prejudicing a new relationship by deciding immediately that you like or dislike a new person. Should you do this, you may be either so "taken in" by one person or so uninterested in another that you cannot think about them as real people.

A quick decision that you like or dislike a person does not give new acquaintances a fair chance. Often you do not even know why you have such feelings about certain individuals. Perhaps your unpremeditated reaction can be traced back to a childhood experience. At that time some people were good to you, and you liked them. Others you feared or disliked. Emotions of love, hate, or fear may have been extended to everything about these persons—color of hair and eyes, tone of voice, mannerisms, dress, ideas. Throughout your life, you may respond to people who resemble them as you earlier responded to them.

If your mother had brown curly hair and blue eyes, perhaps you tend to trust and like every woman who has these characteristics. If the uncle who punished you severely wore a blue suit and had a gruff voice, you may tend to dislike any man who reminds you of him by wearing a blue suit or speaking gruffly. Your love, distrust, or hate really have nothing to do with this new person. You have merely *projected* onto her or him the love or dislike which you had for the first person who walked like that, had eyes like that, or wore clothes like that.

After you have shown your interest in a person and learned to know something about him or her, is is easier to act in ac-

114

cordance with his wishes. This does not mean that you should flatter a person or exploit him for your own selfish ends. It does not mean that you gossip with someone else about a discovery you have made concerning a person. Much unnecessary suffering is caused by thoughtless gossip. If you really care about people, you will become a person whom people can trust. What you wish to cultivate is a sensitiveness to other people's feelings, a genuine consideration of their wishes, a thoughtfulness to prompt all you do and say.

If you remember always that everyone wants a chance to be his or her best, then you will be kind and constructive in any criticism of your friends. You will never let your criticism discourage people. A true friend never needlessly hurts. Neither does she let slip, through cowardice, an occasion when a word from her might help her friend. Because she speaks the truth in love, the edge is taken off unpleasantness. Moreover, with true friends, genuine commendation for something which a person has done well will always accompany any criticism which needs to be made. The affection of a true friend can always be depended on.

In a mature, person-to-person relationship, the joy of life is based, not on demands, but on mutual, spontaneous giving and taking in the things that you do together. This does not mean, however, that you share your deepest thoughts with everyone. Should you do that, you would be in danger of becoming shallow. Neither can it mean that you shut everyone else out of your life because of your dependence on one all-absorbing friendship. No one has the right to have great and intimate friends unless she can also stand alone. Only as you allow yourself to be friends with many people can there be revealed to you the depths and limitations of human nature. Thus can you find yourself.

Mature Friendships

One of the most difficult things for girls to learn is that in adult life relationships change. Time and circumstances make great demands on everyone who wants to live life to the full. This need not mean an end to present friendships, but only a difference in them. Girls need to grow up, to assume the obligations of adults, to carve out their own lives. This each girl must do for herself. She cannot cling, to the point of dependence, to anyone.

What, then, is a mature relationship with people, a mature conception of friendship? Suppose that you are now having a happy relationship with a friend, either a boy or a girl. You see each other daily; you know the joy of constant companionship; you share the many pleasures of friends. When you graduate from school, you need to separate. Although you part and leave each other with sorrow and misgiving, between you there can also be the determination that, because your feeling of friendship is deep, you will find new ways of expressing it. How can you both keep alive that feeling?

First: You can share and identify the beauty around you everywhere with the person whom you care about. You think of and enjoy again the walks and picnics you had together. You cherish a book that you read together. You enjoy visiting a friend whom you both liked. "But," you may say, "remembering past happiness only makes present loneliness more poignant." The loneliness is there. Having the courage to be glad for the joy that preceded it, even though that very joy now causes your loneliness, means that you have found a happiness even deeper than sorrow. Your heart, then, has become more aware of beauty because it is lonely and must look out at the world through the eyes of courage.

116

Friendships are built on informal give-and-take of ideas. Learn to talk interestingly and to listen attentively.

Second: In the work that you both do, you can express the love which binds you together. As each of you discovers the joy and thrill of hard work—even though you have different kinds of jobs in different places, though one of you may be at college, the other at home—you can express, in the way in which you do your job, the joy and thrill of your friendship. Each of you does his or her work well; each knows that he can be proud of the other.

Third: This conviction of yours about the worth of human personality can become the keystone of your life. Because you have cared so deeply for one friend, because that friendship has meant so much to you, you can develop an enduring love for other people. This can become the most important thing in your life—this basic caring about people, this desire

117

to help them to realize their possibilities and "grow up," as your friendship has helped you to do. Then you can never forget your friend. The memory of that friendship never grows dim. Day by day, in all that you do, you are renewing it; you are remembering your friend by living what your friendship has meant to you.

In all your relationships with people, you express this affection. This does not mean that you have a deep, intimate, personal feeling about everyone. However, a concern about people, a conviction of the worth of people, suffuses all your relationships. You hold this as your basic philosophy not because you feel consciously that you must go out and help people but rather because you feel deeply that whatever gives an individual freedom and opportunity for development is to be cherished.

You have gained maturity and strength because you have known the joy of friendship and the pain of readjustment at parting. You are able, therefore, to take the "long view," to come out of any experience with your faith in people unshaken. Though one person may hurt you terribly, though for a while your life seems in ruins and you seem to see only disillusionment, the experience does not leave you bitter. You are still able to believe the truth of the statement that "a friend may prove false, but friendship endures; lovers may break their vows, but love remains; there is much of the divine in the human." You therefore learn to share the burdens of others, to offer your arm for others to lean on. You do not withhold what you have to give through a feeling of your own unworthiness. You do not allow your personal agony to shut out the sufferings of others.

Changes will come in your life as they come to everyone. Will they make friendship more beautiful to you as an enduring value, or will they make it meaningless? Will you shrink from it because the pain of parting cannot be separated from the joy of meeting, thus depriving yourself of a beautiful experience because you are not willing to face the loneliness that is the price you pay for the joy? Or will you take abundance when it is offered to you, recognizing that here is a part of that deep reality which is the essence of life, since it brings both joy and sorrow? Should you choose the second alternative, you will be able to keep friendship always in your life, because always there will be beauty and work and other people.

Communicating with One Another

"I had to talk to somebody who would understand—and you did," the girl told the old friend who gave her the talisman. Most girls will go to great lengths to be heard and understood. They want someone who will see the world as they do, who will marvel with them or comfort them. They are learning that most of us live on little islands of separateness where communication is the strongest link uniting us with our fellow men.

Yet in our crowded, mechanized world, it is hard to communicate with one another. Why is it hard? First, people are different from one another. Often we speak across barriers of nationality, religion, race, politics, even with our families and friends. Mother may have spent her girlhood among the Boston Irish, Father his youth on a Montana ranch; Sister may have married a Mexican; the neighbors may be Italians. Each person differs in what he sees and feels to be important because we understand best what we experience.

Second, communication is difficult when only one person does his part in communicating. Some people want only to speak; they want others to listen to them, but they don't want to hear the other person. Do you ever find yourself waiting impatiently for someone to stop talking so you can begin?

Third, we cannot communicate when we hide from one another. Some people fear contacts with others lest they be hurt by them—or diminished by sharing their lives. They go through the motions of life in a kind of permanent shock, frightened by the rigors of the present, haunted by the past and blind to the future. Truly strong people go about their business *facing things as they must be*. We all need help in understanding the lifetime's experience we have accumulated. When we put our troubles into words and communicate the anger we fear or the love we feel, our tensions relax. Yet some people are afraid to talk to anyone: What will the other person think of me? Will he reject me when he knows my faults? Will I be under obligation to him if I reveal myself? So we hide behind small talk, jokes, silences, false hostility. We say what we think we are supposed to say, not what is really on our minds.

How can you become the kind of person with whom other people *can* talk? Start by learning to listen to people. Next, widen the range of your interests, so that you will have something to say and will understand what people are talking about. Then learn to talk with many different kinds of people, to feel comfortable with them, and to encourage them to share their ideas. Most important, say what you mean. Don't let anyone write your lines for you. Disclose yourself —as you are. When you speak to someone in trust and understanding, real communication between you begins; you have let him know that, despite faults or frailties he may see in himself, you like him and trust your "self" to him.

CHAPTER SIX

Living Happily with Your Family

You SPEND much of your time in your home. It is the most important single influence in your life. There you receive your earliest impressions. There you learn your habits and behavior patterns. Also, home is often the place to which you retreat when you have been hurt or frightened.

Probably more than you realize, the kind of family from which you come, the attitudes of members of your family toward you, the amount and kind of home responsibility that you have, the privileges that you are given, the kind of job that your father has or whether he is unemployed, what other people think of your family, your cultural and nationality background—all of these circumstances of your home life affect the ways in which you act. They also help to explain what makes you different from other girls. As you grasp the significance of each of these factors in your home life, you will understand more clearly the reasons why you behave as you do.

Gaining Independence

The biggest problem that you have to face in gaining independence is your development from a condition of dependence on your parents' care and authority to one of dependence on yourself in making a living, fulfilling your aims and desires, and trusting your own judgment in your behavior. In infancy, you were entirely dependent on grownups for the fulfillment of all of your physical wants. The most that you could do was to signify, by gestures and crying, the nature of your wants, so that others could satisfy them. As you grew older, you learned to satisfy an ever-increasing number of these wants yourself. Such growth is natural, but it is gradual. First you were fed from a bottle; then you were fed from a cup. After a time, you could feed yourself, you could walk, you could dress yourself.

In similar fashion, you should begin early in life gradually to learn to make your own decisions. It is natural for you to want to care for and manage yourself, and it is necessary for you to do so if you are to be a normal adult. However, growth in the ability to make wise decisions comes slowly. You can become emotionally independent of your family only as you learn gradually to make intelligent decisions about day-by-day problems, as you demonstrate your ability to handle your own life wisely.

Some girls like to be babied. Sometimes this process of gaining independence is interrupted. The amount of your dependence on your parents is often explained by your position in the family. It is especially easy to remain dependent if you are a first child, the "baby" of the family, an only child, or an only boy or girl. You may remain immature, also, if you insist that your parents must accompany you everywhere that you go, if you are "nervous," if you have many fears—a fear of the dark, a fear of going to school, a fear of making new acquaintances. You may remain infantile because you have been appealed to on the basis of "Mother needs you"—especially if Father travels and Mother is much alone. Then you stay at home instead of going out to play or going to a party. Probably you do not realize that you are remaining a baby, that you are choosing the easy way out. It may be, on the other hand, that you have been pushed out too fast. Your parents may have been overambitious for you. They may have expected too much of you. Possibly you were not yet ready to be thrust out to stand on your own feet, and you found life so difficult that you were frightened. Therefore, you ran back to the protection of babyhood where you would be taken care of, where your decisions would be made for you.

It may be also that you had an illness and needed to be waited on. Then, because you found such service pleasant, you continued to demand it. Some girls so enjoy being waited on that they become pampered. They expect their mothers to bring them their breakfasts in bed, pick up their clothes, polish their shoes, or wash their stockings for them. On the other hand, some girls may have a physical inferiority upon which they capitalize and because of which they allow themselves to be babied. They are afraid to leave the protection of their homes, because other people might tease or pity them because of the handicap—or just because "people always notice it."

Some parents like to pamper girls. Sometimes mothers enjoy waiting on their children. They do not force them to grow up, as mother birds do when they push their babies out of the nests to force them to fly. Mothers may think that they are being kind to a girl when they do the housework that has been designated for the girl, or when they make too many of a girl's decisions for her. They want to make life easier for their children. Love of their children is the basis for this oversolicitude, but this is unwise love. Parents who step in to carry the responsibility for a girl's mistakes so that she will not be hurt—or who make her decisions for her so that she will not make mistakes—should know that everyone needs to feel the consequences of one's own mistakes; everyone must learn to take responsibility for one's own actions if one is to be able to face the world with confidence. Unless a girl is given these opportunities, she may, for the rest of her life, run back to mother and father when she has been hurt or when she cannot make a decision. She will do this not because she "loves" her mother and father but because she needs them; she is overdependent on them.

How Dependent Are You?

The measure of a girl's dependence on her parents is: How many areas of her life do they control? Of course she should listen to their advice, but how many times does she accept their decisions because she is too lazy or too immature to think through a problem herself? Do her parents tell her what job she may take? Do they select her friends? Is she prejudiced against marriage because her parents have told her about so many unhappy ones or because their own marriage was unhappy? Is she reluctant to go with boys because

124

she cannot find any like her father or because her mother criticizes those with whom she does go, telling her that they are uncouth or not good enough for her, that women are superior, or that she should wait for an interesting man? Does she choose her own boy companions, or does she wait for her mother to pick one out for her? Does her mother make it so pleasant for a girl at home—perhaps not even asking her to do any household tasks—that the girl loses her desire to try the unfamiliar?

If a girl remains dependent on her family in too many of these particular ways, she may become the kind of woman who, later in life, has few friends, because she has never learned to trust or to feel comfortable with anyone outside of her family. Such a woman may be unhappy and unsuited to a job because she had no part in choosing it. She may never marry, because she is so "grateful" to her parents for all that they have done or because she thinks her parents need her to support them. She may even remain single and at home because her mother or father appealed to her on the basis of "If you loved me, you wouldn't care about him— or about that job!"

How to Gain More Independence

Sometimes a girl becomes very impatient with her parents when she finds that she is more ready for responsibilities and independence than her parents are to give them to her. If a girl tries honestly to see why her parents feel as they do, if she tries to understand what makes them the kind of people they are, or if she tries to figure out why she wants what she does, she may discover that her parents have a realistic basis for their hesitation.

In Chapter 5 it was shown that every person needs to feel wanted. It is natural for your parents, also, to enjoy feeling that you need them. Moreover, they have, over a good many years, developed habits of doing things for you. When you were a helpless child, their care and protection were necessary for your very life. Strong habits are not easily broken. Certainly parents will not break them unless they are assured that your ability to take care of yourself will supplant their care of you and that they need have no fear of what may happen to you when you venture into the world alone. Occasionally a girl may feel, however, that her parents' concern about her is actually a desire to hold on to her and that her parents are, although they aren't aware of it, doing the unfair thing to keep from losing her. Even this is understandable.

It is really quite an adjustment for parents to make when they find that you seem to need them less and less as you grow up. The adjustment is something like that which a movie star must make when she finds her popularity waning and she must move off the center of the stage because her place has gradually been usurped by other people. After all, does anyone else have a more legitimate right to be concerned about you than your parents? From the point of view of cold facts alone, your parents have made quite an investment in you. No one allows his investments to fail without making some attempts to save them. You might attempt to figure up sometime how much you have cost, in dollars alone, from the time when you came, a tiny baby, into the home of which you are now a part. The total would be a staggering amount—thousands of dollars. Add to that all the time and care that your physical well-being alone has demanded. People have had to spend hours in tasks for you that they could have spent in doing things for themselves. For instance, someone has had to wash your clothes thousands of times, feed you, and dress you. A person, you see, is a valuable article. Do you wonder, then, that your parents are afraid of what may happen to you?

Your parents are especially afraid for you if they feel that they do not know you very well because you have not talked with them about yourself. They are particularly careful if the family has recently moved and they feel that they do not know a community well. Or if they were born in another country, they may feel an ocean, as well as a generation, removed from you. In the latter case, they are less sure than ever of your standards, because these are so different from the only ones that they know. Your parents may then even be afraid about your clothes, your amusements, and especially the fact that you go around with boys.

Many parents may also be afraid of what may happen to a girl if they think that she has inadequate sex information. In their day, perhaps they did not talk about such things; therefore, they cannot give her information; they do not know how to or they are too embarrassed to talk. Consequently, they try to protect her in the only way they know—by using their authority over her to forbid her to do whatever they consider dangerous.

When parental attitudes such as these confront you, what do you do? Are you a good or a poor investment? Do you rebel and loudly demand all your independence at once? Do you escape into daydreams where you can have all the things you want? Do you take revenge on your parents by becoming jealous, by hating, or by stealing, in order to prove

127

that you can assert yourself in some fashion? Or do you try honestly to figure out what the grown-up way of acting would be in your situation?

Make it possible for your parents to meet and know your friends.

What is it that you really want in your family relationship? Above all else, you want to feel secure. You need to feel that you belong in some group, that you are accepted and loved just as you are, with your faults as well as your abilities. Your home should be the place where, more than anywhere else, you feel safe. The security that you have in the knowledge that you belong somewhere, that you are greatly loved, is

128

the starting point in your growth. To feel secure in your family relationship is especially important now when insecurity in many other areas is so prevalent and when technological changes are occurring so rapidly that you cannot foretell what your future may be—or even whether there will be a future! In these times, it is comforting to realize that family life has gone on for centuries, although, naturally, the form which it assumes has changed. Your parents furnish you a home. It was because they wanted someone in that home to love and to care for that you came into the world. They furnish you indispensable security in their love. Their unfailing belief in you gives you the courage to grow up.

However, along with your desire for security, you have the drive toward independence, the need to develop initiative and a sense of responsibility. Girls sometimes think that these two desires cannot be reconciled. They cause themselves and their families great unhappiness by repeatedly attempting to do what they call "asserting their independence," so as to demonstrate to their families that they are grown-up. The truly mature person knows that no individual can ever be really independent of everyone else. No matter where one is in life, one must learn the combination of obeying reasonable commands and taking initiative and responsibility for one's own words and actions. The mature person sees herself not only as an individual but as a member of a family and of a community. She knows that, in order to gain the security that comes from feeling herself a part of a group, she must cooperate with the other members of the group in working out means by which all can live together harmoniously.

Many girls get along very happily with their families. They have helped to create in their homes a respect for the

129

individuality of each member of the family group, as well as a basic understanding among the various members of the family which no disagreement can ever destroy, although individual members of the group may differ with one another, or even quarrel. If you will help to work out such a relationship, your reward will be your family's confidence in you and respect for you.

How can you develop such an attitude? There are very positive types of behavior that you can work out in your family group. Some have already been discussed. If the cause of your remaining a baby, of being cared for, is a physical handicap or a feeling of social inadequacy, confront your problem. Do something about it if you can. If you cannot, do not feel hurt if people notice it. Compensate for it in as large a measure as possible; then go out and face the world instead of hiding in your home. Grow up. If you are being kept a baby on the basis of the appeal "If you love me, you won't do that," do not sulk or rage. Talk the problem over with your parents. Help them gradually to see that it is not a question of your love for them. Give them the assurance that they do have your love and will always have it. Help them to recognize that the real question is, for example, whether you will be able, later in life, to choose friends intelligently, to throw yourself wholeheartedly into your work. In order to grow up, you must learn to depend on yourself by making an increasing number of your own decisions now.

The basis of all family relationships must be a genuine interest in, as well as a careful consideration of, the wishes of every member of the family group. Many families have found useful the idea of holding a weekly family discussion in which the opinions of every member of the family are heard and genuine consideration given them. Real and honest discussion of family problems can be a safety valve to ease the irritation that a girl occasionally feels toward her family. She may be concerned because her parents have asked her to abide by rules of conduct which she resents because she does not understand them and her parents have never explained to her the reasons for them. A girl may feel that she does not have a sufficiently large allowance. She may believe that her little brother is being favored by her mother at her expense. It is in the frank discussion of problems such as these that weekly family gatherings contribute toward the reduction of possible friction in the family.

Suppose that we look at the question of rules of conduct, for instance. A girl may be unhappy because there is no agreement within the family circle as to the standards expected of her. Therefore, she adopts those which leave her freest, with the result that one parent defends the girl against the other parent, while the girl feels uncomfortable and on the defensive with one parent. On the other hand, both parents may agree on rules, but their rules may be so different from the standards adopted by the girl's own group of friends, to which she feels that she must conform if she is to have friends and fun, that she either defies her parents, doing as she chooses and becoming secretive about her actions, or remains at home alone rather than run the risk of being different and unpopular with a group of her contemporaries.

How much wiser a procedure it would be to present this matter in a family discussion! The girl could elaborate her point of view. Her parents would have an opportunity to explain their standards and perhaps help her to gain a sense of perspective about social expectations. Her parents might see, also, the importance of their all agreeing on such matters as the kinds of friends a girl is to have, the age at which she is to be allowed to drive the family car, the hour at which she is to come home after a date, the number of dates that she is to have in a week. Parents and girl together might, each with an open mind, discuss the reason for certain rules that a girl finds particularly difficult to keep. After such a discussion, either the parents might see the wisdom of modifying a particular rule if they can advance no good reason for the girl's obeying it, or the girl might recognize that her parents had a very valid motive for their command. The discussion might end by the entire group deciding upon a few rules which seem valuable and which the girl wants to keep because she sees why it is important that she do so.

As a result of such discussion, parents may also have their attention called to the fact that sometimes they make a girl's life difficult by too much emphasis on matters which, in the long run, may be comparatively unimportant, such as a girl's awkwardness, her great concern over clothes, her occasional choice of friends of whom they do not approve. On the other hand, a girl may recognize that her own too great concern over these matters is primarily a reaction to a stage in her growth when she feels insecure "all over": when her hands and feet are too large for her; when she has not yet developed assurance about the kind of clothes she can wear; when she is uncertain whether she is accepted by her social group; when she has not yet learned the proper thing to do and say in a variety of situations. As she grows up physically, socially, and emotionally, she gains experience and confidence in

132

these areas. Then she understands that she was once unduly concerned and sensitive about her temporary inadequacies.

If the question at issue is that of the girl's friendships with boys or girls of whom the family does not approve, she might face the question of what the basis of her friendship is. A girl needs many different kinds of friends. Some friends may teach her new skills; others may symbolize security in her social group. For example, the girl at whose home she is spending so many afternoons, the girl to whose flashy clothes and loud voice her mother objects, may be very important to a girl because this friend is teaching her the newest dance steps. The boy who may seem rough and uncouth to adults is going to be the school's football captain next year, and the girl may be the envy of her classmates because she is dating him, although she might reluctantly admit that, under other circumstances, she might not find him so attractive.

A girl needs to remember that, during her high school days, she is only in the process of discovering what she actually expects of her friends. There will be much trial and error before she finds out what kinds of people she really likes. She will make and break many of her friendships, unless she prolongs them because she enjoys the furor that she creates in the family and the attention that her parents give her by their repeated and vociferous objections to a particular friend of the moment!

One indication of a girl's progress toward maturity is her ability to recognize that a mature person is not one who conforms in all details to the standards of her companions. A mature girl does not need to be governed entirely by her friends' behavior in order to be accepted and liked. She will recognize, on the other hand, that certain peculiarities of behavior, which are annoying to a group with whom she lives as intimately as she does with her family group, must be ironed out if she is to live happily either with them now or in her own home later in life.

If a girl is the kind of person who gets attention from her parents by continually teasing or ridiculing her younger brothers and sisters, she will find a more constructive occupation in learning about child development—in observing her younger brothers and sisters from the point of view of learning about the behavior of young children, much as adults often observe nursery school children in order to prepare themselves for professional work in dealing with children of that age.

Again, a girl might build up standards of what her contribution to a happy family life could be if she suggested, in a family discussion, that everyone consider the characteristics and actions of an ideal son or daughter. Then, if everyone responds good-naturedly to this discussion, the family might be willing to proceed to a consideration of the ideal mother, father, unmarried aunt, or grandmother.

If you feel annoyed because you believe that your parents are not giving you a fair allowance, perhaps you can request that the family budget be one of the items discussed by the family. Do not, however make your request in an irritable or injured manner, as though your wants were the family's most important consideration. You might suggest that you would be willing to do some special family chores or take care of the younger children to earn some extra money, if extra money is available. If you display willingness to understand your parents' financial problems, they might be willing to be

134

frank with you about the amount of money actually coming into the house every week. In fact, your parents might even suggest that the entire family work out a family budget. Then all the family together might discuss the wants of all its members and decide how far the money will go. Sometimes the family will decide that there is enough money this week to pay for the shoes you need, but that you must wait until next month for another new dress. Again, you may all decide together that it is more important to take your brother the dentist at once than to buy your new sports shoes. If the entire family discusses a problem, no one person is likely to resent the decision. Each person has had a part in making it.

One word of caution about these family gatherings! They should be discussions, not debates. They should be a sharing of ideas with consideration of everyone's point of view, not the imposition of the ideas of the person who can talk the loudest. If you wish your family to treat you as an adult, you must act like one. You cannot insist upon your own way or have a temper tantrum during one of these family conferences when you do not get what you want. Listen to your parents' reasons for the requests they make—don't just shout your reasons for objecting. Try to see the situation from their point of view.

Show your family that you have some good ideas, that you can exercise mature judgment, that you can make a real contribution toward the solution of problems that trouble the entire family. They may be surprised to discover how grown-up you are. You will have demonstrated that you are a person to be reckoned with, that you can no longer be treated as a baby.

Develop your parents' confidence in you. You might attempt to develop some interests in common with other family members by doing at least one thing with each individual member of your family which you will both enjoy. This is more difficult now than it was a hundred years ago. In those days, the home was the center of all of life. Members of the family had many interests in common. They all had to do a variety of things together to keep the family going, from piecing quilts to making candles. The home was the center of amusements in which the entire family had a part. Now each member of the family may have a different interest. Each may go to a different school, work at a different kind of job. Most of the clothes and food are bought outside of the home. For amusement, Father reads the newspapers, Mother watches TV, brother goes to the movies, and sister is off to a dance.

Under such circumstances, it is difficult to build up interests in common, but it is possible if everyone tries. Recently a high school girl gave a dance in the family basement, which she and her father and brothers had decorated and painted. For the furnishings, they repaired old furniture contributed by their neighbors and friends. Later, her brother put up a billiard table, and her older sister set up a table for Pingpong. However, a girl need not do anything so elaborate as this. If she really feels a kindly interest in her parents and in other members of the family she can, perhaps, show it by hiking with her brother, by discussing politics and news events with Father, by playing cards or by sharing a book she has enjoyed with Mother, by talking at home about people who interest her, by keeping an attitude of frankness about all that she does, by sharing confidences with her parents. They may not demand a girl's confidence—certainly

136

you would resent it if they "pumped" you—but you know that they are eager to have you talk to them. They want to know how you are thinking and what you are thinking. In these simple and natural ways, a girl makes it possible for her parents to enjoy her comradeship, and she also builds up their confidence in her and in her judgment.

It takes time, however, to build up your parents' confidence in you; it cannot be done overnight, or even in a year. If you think that you are not being given sufficient independence because your parents are not convinced that you are ready for the next step, you must be able to demonstrate to them that you have acquired the capacity for making wise decisions. You do this by keeping your promises, accepting your responsibilities, exercising mature judgment, and taking the consequences of your mistakes. When you have promised to abide by certain rules, keep your promises. If you have agreed to come in at eleven, don't arrive at two. Come in a little earlier than the hour set. Thus your parents learn that they can trust you, and incidentally it will be easier for you to secure permission to go out the next time you want to do so. Be frank with your parents. Tell them where you are going and with whom. Make it possible for them to meet your friends, and show them that you are eager to have your friends meet them. Then you will usually have no difficulty gaining permission to go out with your friends!

Another way in which you can demonstrate to your parents that you can accept responsibility for yourself is by going through the routine of the day without having them repeatedly checking on you. You can get up alone. You do not have to be reminded to clean your room, to do the household tasks which have been assigned to you, to do your homework, to have your clothes ready for school the next day, or

137

Learn about books, sports, politics, and what is going on in the world.

to be in bed at the hour agreed upon. You exercise good judgment in the way in which you use money, spend your leisure time, choose your clothes, and select your friends. This behavior assures your parents that you do have desirable goals and ambitions for your life, that you do have high standards, and that you know what you want to get out of life.

138

When you make mistakes in judgment, you take the consequences without whimpering. You do not expect your parents to make good your mistakes. Often it is through your own errors that you realize the wisdom of your parents' judgment; you may discover that they were wise where you were mistaken. It is through mistakes that you learn to use better judgment the next time. However, you must expect your parents to try to prevent your making mistakes that will have too serious consequences.

Your parents can relinquish their authority over you only when they are convinced that you have replaced outside authority by inner authority—namely, your own intelligent judgment. If, as you are growing up, you can also build up a genuine comradeship with your parents, you and they will both find this relationship very satisfying.

The Question of Discipline

If attitudes of understanding and mutual respect prevail in your home, then the next big question—that of family authority, or discipline—is not a severe problem with you. Discipline in a family group should be thought of as a method of guiding a responsible person, rather than as punishment or domination. It need not be resented. Its basis should be the mutual respect of parent and daughter for one another. The girl can use it as a means to help her make an honest attempt not only to live up to standards which she understands and has accepted but also to develop a sense of responsibility for her own actions. Discipline is valuable because it gives guidance in developing life patterns.

Often girls resent their parents' method of disciplining them because they cannot understand it. They quickly become impatient, their parents become impatient, and then there is a clash. One girl showed a good deal of discernment when she said, "When Mother is tired, she yells at me."

Uncertainty as to the result of an action often explains your reaction to discipline. If sometimes you are punished severely for disobeying or making a mistake and at other times the incident passes without any comment—your parents' behavior being dependent upon the mood of the moment or upon their own disagreement about the severity of your punishment—your behavior may become unpredictable. You may become nervous, irritable, and unhappy. On the one hand, you may take a chance and do something which another girl would not risk doing because she would be certain that punishment would follow. Again, you may learn to play up to parental moods. You may have discovered that sometimes if you tease long enough for something, you get it but at other times this doesn't work. So you wait for a "good mood." Such a situation results in a chronic state of uncertainty as to what will happen to you.

If you have had a fear of punishment and authority built up in you or if you have been told that you must always obey and never question why, then you are likely to do one of two things: First, you may rebel openly and refuse to obey. Then you may get the reply "I'll *make* you do it. I'll break your stubborn will." There may be raised voices and flushed faces; you may be called names, slapped, or punished even more strenuously. Second, you may submit protestingly, but slink off and make up your mind to climb on top of the world somehow, even if it has to be by bullying your little brother or sister or by bossing the club. Perhaps you may have been shamed into submission—been told how "bad" you were, have had to listen to the story of your "badness" told to someone else in front of you so that you would remember to be ashamed. Again, you may have been told that you should be "grateful" for all that your family did for you, or that your conduct made Mother or Father feel so bad. Perhaps they have even cried. It may be that you have been nagged into submission, or you may have been frightened by "What will the neighbors think?"

Unless you understand and evaluate this kind of discipline, you may build up a fear of all authority, no matter where throughout life you find it. You may be afraid to talk to the teacher or afraid to approach a prospective employer because you cannot talk in a natural way to anyone who might be in authority over you. On the other hand, such a method of disciplining may make you bitter, resentful of any authority, eager to get your revenge on someone because advantage has been taken of your helplessness and immaturity. You may become the kind of person who, throughout life, resists authority, takes pride in "getting by," in "putting something over," or resents and breaks any rules that restrict what you call your "freedom." Again, this type of discipline may crush you, take away from you the power to think for yourself. You may have had "duty" to others, the "right" thing to do, and even religious doctrines all brought in to reinforce the statement that your ideas were inferior to those of your elders. They may have said that you are not smart enough to have such "big ideas" or that you think you are too smart and will "get your head bumped." Even though you may have tried, by rebelling openly, to convince others that such

141

accusations had no effect on you, you may go around the rest of your life trying to convince yourself that what has been said about you is not true.

This type of discipline becomes especially dangerous if, as you grow up, you honestly disagree with your parents about educational standards, religion, or relationships with boys. Then your parents may become frightened and attempt more than ever to convince you that they are right. They may ridicule and in every possible way try to belittle your ideas. You, in turn, may retaliate by planning to throw overboard "as soon as I'm grown up" your parents' advice and commands, their traditions, their moral codes, and their religious teachings.

Get whatever good you can from discipline. Should this be your family experience, can you be mature enough in your attitude toward it to profit by it instead of becoming bitter or crushed by it? A baby might yell, "I want what I want when I want it." See whether you, on the other hand, can take the attitude "I shall not attempt to assert my independence all at once but shall do so gradually as I become surer of my own standards. My family experience can teach me a great deal. The better I learn how to meet my difficulties here, the better equipped I am to meet them in the world." If you can develop such a point of view, you will have learned how to take a positive attitude toward life. You will have applied your energies—set your will—to help yourself. You will be growing up.

It is not necessary, no matter how difficult your family experiences, that you develop indecision, self-consciousness, dependence, and self-distrust—all of which show in you

142

either when you act like a frightened, crushed child, a perpetual doormat of whom anyone may take advantage, or a "hard-boiled," overaggressive individual who talks the loudest about the things of which she is least certain or pushes herself forward on all occasions to convince herself that she counts.

You are not exhibiting a mature attitude toward your difficulties if you go around for the remainder of your life being afraid of getting slapped! Should you do so, you may become the kind of girl who has good ideas but who always gets someone else to volunteer them, who cannot express her own opinions or stand on her own feet. If you have been shamed, you need not go around always being terrified of people, afraid to make friends, afraid that you are not as good as someone else, afraid that there is something queer about you—you "just know" that people are talking about you.

If you govern all details of your behavior by what you think other people may think about you, you may never be able to see an issue clearly. You may try, for instance, to become the kind of person whom you think that your friend of the moment likes, instead of being the kind of person you yourself would like to be. You may try to do exactly what you think your friend admires and wants; you copy her clothes, her mannerisms, and her actions.

It is dangerous, also, to acquire such fear of another person's emotions, of someone else's rages or nagging or crying, that you cannot be natural with people and cannot enjoy them. If you become too fearful of authority, then all through your life you may tend to fear anyone in authority over you.

You may develop the idea that this person is there only to criticize you or to blame you. You attempt to be careful when he or she is around; you attempt to make an impression, yet you succeed only in being nervous and in doing everything wrong. Actually, this person may be trying his or her best to help you. Such a fear makes you unfair to people; it gives you an unreal conception of authority. It destroys your self-confidence, because no matter what you are doing and how well you are doing it, your attention is focused not on your task but on what someone else is thinking about you and the way in which you are doing the job at hand.

If your behavior inside your family group and outside is being governed by emotions such as these—feelings which have developed out of a fear of punishment—be honest enough to admit that you may be acting in an infantile fashion and making a poor adjustment. You do not need, because of unfortunate experiences in your family, either to rebel, to escape into an unreal world, or to condemn the world in which you find yourself. Try to look at this quarreling, these attempts to discipline you for your mistakes, as learning points for you on the road to growing up, not as irreparable errors for which you need to feel inferior or as wrongs for which you must secure revenge.

Make discipline less necessary. There are many attitudes which, if cultivated in your family group, would make a show of authority by your parents less necessary. Several suggestions have already been made. Others might be made with regard to your relationships with your brothers and sisters. Do you try to take out on them the punishment that your parents have given you? If you do, you need not be surprised if they retaliate by tattling on you at their earliest

144

opportunity or if their jealousy and desire to dominate come out in teasing you. Sometimes the teasing is done merely to "get a rise" out of you. This is the time to ignore teasing and not let it bother you.

Have you realized and accepted the necessity of your parents' sharing their love and all the family possessions among all of the children? Or do you ask for more than your share of money, clothes, or attention? Then do you attempt to defend yourself by saying that one child is favored more than another because one is smarter, more talented, or so much like someone whom the parent likes? It may be true that one child is favored. It may even be true that, in a moment of exasperation, one parent may have told you that you were bad or stubborn or not reliable. You translated this to mean that you are neglected and unwanted. You may go to all lengths of self-pity in this delusion, even to planning your own funeral, comforting yourself that "then they'll be sorry" that they did not appreciate you.

If you can cultivate a healthy respect for private property, many quarrels will be avoided, and there will be fewer occasions when discipline is necessary. No one likes to have her jewelry or clothes worn without her permission, her money borrowed and not repaid, or her dresser drawer upset because you wanted to find a head scarf. If you remember, also, to be courteous to, and considerate of, other members of the household, you will be more likely to receive that same kind of consideration in return. If you assume your share of responsibility in the household tasks and care of the children, you will be proving to your parents that you are able to assume responsibility for guiding your own life and for making your own decisions.

Make the Most of Your Background

There may be other conditions inherent in your family background that can make life very difficult for you if you allow them to "get you down." You may not like the house that you live in; you may have no convenient place to entertain friends, or even to study. You may not like your neighborhood. You may feel that your family is looked down upon because of the kind of work your father does, because he is unemployed, or because you are of a different nationality or religion or color from that of most of the girls whom you know at school. A great many girls are faced with circumstances such as these. There are, for instance, millions of boys and girls in this country whose parents were born in other countries. Puerto Ricans, Cubans, Mexicans, Europeans, Orientals—immigrants from every continent have sought new homes and lives here. Many boys and girls are unhappy about the homes and the neighborhoods in which they live. Adequate housing at reasonable cost is one of the greatest problems facing our country. Many young people come from homes that do not have an income sufficient to provide a comfortable standard of living. Economic insecurity and fear of the future are not unusual.

If any or all of these factors apply to you, you may develop a feeling of inferiority. You may think of yourself as severely handicapped and, consequently, inferior to other girls. You may not be able to look people in the eye. You may be always afraid that someone will insult you. You may become loud and vulgar and antisocial. On the other hand, you can use any handicap, real or imagined, to spur you on to greater efforts in demonstrating the ability that you do have. You can find some positive factor in each of these difficulties.

If, for example, girls of other nationalities are sometimes so unkind and so unsympathetic to your nationality that they call you names which they have heard from ill-mannered adults, try to be big enough so that the things they say do not hurt you. It is not necessary to hit back at these people, to slink into a hole, or to become tough. Such people are merely playing on your fear of being different. And what a dull world this would be if we all had to be alike! Do not allow yourself to cultivate the feeling that you are confronting a problem about which you can do nothing. See it as a part of the larger problem that other girls are facing all over the country, and work out what your contribution to its solution can be.

If this is your problem, you, yourself, can deeply appreciate and help other Americans to appreciate the contributions that the representatives of your family's culture have made to this country. You can develop a profound respect for the culture that your parents represent. This does not mean that you run back to the old culture, customs, and point of view to escape hurt in the new, but rather that you accept the challenge to find out what you can add from the old to enrich the new. In this way, both cultures richly endow your life.

Ask your parents or grandparents to tell you something of the background and cultural heritage of the country that they knew. Then you yourself will feel a thrill at what it means to be a member of the national group from which they came. Learn what you can of that country's language, history, folk tales, handicrafts, music, and dances. Find out what people of your family's nationality who came to America have contributed to this country in developing its

147

industry, science, art, and so on. Be proud of their achievements and generous about sharing your social inheritance in groups of which you are a part. If you can learn a second language at home, do so. You are fortunate. Most Americans speak only one language and many girls struggle to learn a second one because they see the need for it. They will envy you your language facility.

At home, a girl takes her first steps toward learning to guide her own life. If you rely too closely upon the protection, help, and standards of your family, you will never learn to think for yourself or to act upon your own decisions. Conversely, if you revolt suddenly and completely from your family, you lose the valuable social heritage that your parents can pass on to you. If they were born in another culture, their values may differ from those you are learning from your friends and your school. You may sometimes feel superior to your parents because their values do not fit the American pattern. You may drift between their standards and yours; or you may become antisocial and find it difficult to accept authority of any kind without extreme irritation. If you are really grown-up, you will understand that many values are not permanent; they grow out of what makes sense in a given culture at a given time. There is nothing permanent in this world but change. If you are perceptive, you will see the wisdom of some of your parents' values, like their belief in self-reliance and in a closely knit family group in which everyone feels accepted and secure.

Do You Need Parents?

"Teen-agers are also parent-agers" was one Father's weary verdict after a loud confrontation with his daughter. "Sometimes I think they don't need parents—they are so worldly and well informed. But they're not grown-up enough to recognize that there is much they don't know, so there are times when I say, 'Do this. I know for sure.' They resent my intruding on their 'freedom,' but I'm giving them freedom—to try out the limits I set! If they can convince me that they're ready for wider limits, more power to them!"

Some parents disagree with this father. They think that parents should say "I don't know," rather than "Do this. I know for sure." They believe that the "battle" between parents and teen-agers should be "called off." Younger parents, particularly, say that they intend to love, not discipline, their children; that they plan to teach them independence early and not impose themselves or their ideas. What do teen-agers respond?

Patti and other girls have said wistfully, "Our family is just a bunch of people who live under one roof. We go about our own business. Sometimes I'd like to talk to my parents and find out what they really believe in. They must expect something of me. But I don't know what until I've done something they don't like and they say I've disappointed them— I don't get any authority at home. I don't think it's fair. I feel like I'm driving a car through traffic with no stop signs around." Being given no direction apparently leaves girls angry, frightened, bewildered. Why?

Girls need to feel secure—to feel wanted and accepted in their homes. If their parents leave them without guidance, girls can feel that their parents don't care enough about them to take the time and thought to guide them. Parents may think that they are being kind; they don't know all the answers, so they don't want to dictate or be too hard on girls. The result is an impasse; parents fail to communicate anything, and their silence is interpreted as neglect or lack of

149

concern. Some girls respond to this situation by dramatic behavior or delinquent acts which force their parents to "take over" and pay attention to them. Other girls, cut off from their parents, withdraw into the society of their peers. Here they get their tastes and values which then may be criticized by the very parents who abdicated their responsibility and dumped teen-agers into a society composed only of their peers. Every girl's ultimate goal is to find her place in adult society. If she feels shut off from the adult world just when she is on the verge of entering it, and needs confidence, she will cling fiercely to members of her own generation. Thus there can develop a widening gap between teen-agers and adults, even the "separate society" notion!

Many parents are aware of this lack of communication. Some girls report that their parents have questioned them anxiously, "What did I do wrong?" How would you answer this question? First, face the fact that you *do* need parents; girls need assurance that their parents care about them, accept them, and want them. Parents' trust and approval, in turn, develops assurance that society will accept them and place confidence in them. Second, you need imagination: "What would it be like to be a parent who has the responsibility for me and my behavior?" Third, you need perspective: "If I were in my parents' shoes, how would I help me grow up?" Fourth, you need humor: "Of course, from my point of view, the best parents are never quite good enough!" Given such understanding of your parents' dilemma, you can come halfway, maybe more, to start real communication.

The important thing is to continue discussing and listening to each other's point of view. Though you will not always agree, the heart of the matter for each is understanding why the other disagrees. There will be basic disagreements for

150

several reasons. First, you and your parents may be very different people. Your temperament may be more like grandma's or Aunt Lucy's than like mother's; in fact, you might have felt more at home with other parents. But this is the family to which you were born; it's up to you to learn give-and-take here! Second, your parents are people too, with handicaps, fears, and prejudices absorbed from their early environment. Consequently, they will have periods of stress and strain when they are preoccupied with their own problems and show little inclination to become involved with yours. Third, a mature adult's perspective on his needs and desires is different from yours. One who has learned to postpone his wants for other people's sometimes becomes impatient with your insistent needs and desires. Or he may have forgotten what it was like to want something desperately, urgently—now! Fourth, the world you live in comprises more than your family. Parents' expectations sometimes may be the exact opposite of those of your friends. How do you resolve the situation when your parents expect behavior for which your friends would jeer at you? Fifth, your parents know that you have the right to grow up, to grow away from them. They may *want* you to grow up; but it is difficult to "let go." You, on the other hand, will not become an adult simply by growing bigger; you must break the ties of dependence. This is especially difficult if you find that you are losing your parents' confidence because your ambitions, dreams, and thoughts differ from theirs. You may have to "get rough" to break free and give yourself a chance at a life which is not a carbon copy of theirs. Your confidence in yourself may reawaken their confidence in you.

CHAPTER SEVEN

Building Friendships with Boys

"High school girls aren't interested in anything except themselves and their boy friends—how you get one, what you do when you're with him, how you keep him," one high school girl complained ruefully. These matters do occupy a good many minutes of the waking hours of many girls. It is natural that this should be true. High school girls are growing up emotionally; they need to know boys—how to make their acquaintance, how to make themselves attractive to them, how to associate happily with them. Girls see their companionship with boys in school as an opportunity to extend their experience and knowledge about people in general, and about the opposite sex in particular, so that they may, in time, know how to select a husband and have their own family.

Going Out with Boys

Is there a definite age at which a girl is suddenly old enough to go out with boys? Most wise adults have discovered that there is not. The fortunate girl is the one who has known, played, and fought with boys all her life. Then, as she begins to grow up, to mature physically, she feels a new attraction to boys. She may be excited and disturbed about them, yet shy or a little scornful of them. Also, since a boy usually develops physically about two years later than a girl, some boys her own age may seem crude or awkward or silly to her.

As a girl becomes interested in boys, she expresses this interest in her behavior. She wants to have pretty clothes. She is concerned with the appearance of her hair, her skin, her fingernails. She spends hours in front of the mirror. She likes romantic stories in books and magazines and movies. Her family, especially younger brothers and sisters, may tease and ridicule her about some of her new interests. One way for her to minimize the teasing is to ignore it.

In order to make life at home as easy as possible at this stage, a girl should remember to go slowly in her wants. If she demands more than her share of the spending money available or asks for too many new clothes, she need not be surprised if brothers and sisters are jealous of her and make life miserable for her. If she wants permission to stay out late too many nights or to have too many parties, her parents will become impatient with her, may restrain her by means of their authority, or may become genuinely concerned because she, as a growing girl, is not having enough rest.

When parents object. Sometimes a girl's parents are not eager to have her go out with boys; they may not even like it when a boy calls her up. When he comes to see her, they may find many things wrong with him. He may not make a good impression because he has not learned how to wear his clothes. He may not seem interesting. When parents are critical, they are sometimes making a direct appeal to the girl's love for them. They may want to keep her at home because they are reluctant to see her grow up and perhaps marry and leave their home to establish one of her own. At these times, a girl needs to be particularly considerate of her parents. She should let them know that they count in her life.

She should be careful, however, not to dismiss too easily her parents' comments about her boy friends. Because of their longer experience with people, parents are often able to discern qualities which the girl, too, will learn in time and by experience to recognize. Meanwhile, she will be wise to capitalize on her parents' experience.

But what can she do if her parents definitely object to her going out with any boys at all? She may have to recognize that some of their attitudes will be very difficult to change. Her best course in such a situation is to find out what the basis of their objection is. It may be the fact that they have no confidence in her. Perhaps they fear that she does not know how to choose friends. Or perhaps she has made unreasonable demands or broken promises she made them.

How can a girl build up her parents' trust in her? One way to develop her parents' confidence in her and her friends is to bring her friends home to introduce them to her parents, to have parties or entertain at home, so that her parents have a chance to meet her friends. Thus her parents gradually gain assurance that she knows how to choose her friends. A wise girl is careful not to make what most parents consider impossible demands, such as a date every night. She also keeps her promises; for example, she comes home when she says she will. Incidentally, a boy does not respect a girl any more because she stays out late with him. Sometimes he respects her less.

Another reason why parents may object to a girl's going

out with boys is that they fear she has insufficient knowledge of sex. Even if your parents feel that they cannot give this information to you themselves, it is possible for you to secure it. Ask an older friend—a teacher, a counselor, or a doctor—to suggest a book on the subject. Good ones are usually found in school libraries. Discuss your reading with your mother, if possible. If you cannot, at least let her know what you have read, and let her know who recommended it to you. If sex education is given to you in a course at school, let your parents know this. It may reassure them.

Sometimes parents object to having their daughter go out with boys because they have been brought up according to customs of some other country or community or do not understand the customs in your high school. In such a situation, an older friend might be of help. This friend must, of course, be a person who is patient, who appreciates the background of your parents, who can interpret the customs of your school and community and thus soothe your parents' fears.

Usually some solution can gradually be arrived at if a girl is willing to work out her problem with tact and understanding. In the meantime she will be content with seeing boys wherever possible—in classes and activities in school and church, or at the homes of her friends. On the other hand, a girl may refuse to think through her problem. She may remain at home, making no effort to know boys. She may even become "sour grapes" on boys. Again, a girl may lose patience, rebel, and make her life a constant succession of scenes. Which of these choices promises the best results?

Getting acquainted. Be friendly with boys. Smile at them; know what to talk about with them; discover a common interest. How do you begin? Often you can make the first approach to a boy by asking him an intelligent question about

155

something in which you know that he is interested. He never labels that "chasing after" him. You are chasing him only when you resort to baby tricks, like giggling or calling him repeatedly on the telephone, to attract his attention.

Be yourself when you talk with a boy. Concentrate on making *him* feel happy and comfortable.

There are many opportunities for meeting boys. Talk to them in homeroom and class; become a part of school activities; join school clubs; work on committees; go to class parties and dances. Take advantage of opportunities offered through churches and community clubs. Make friends with boys and girls at parties. A girl friend or an older friend can often introduce you to a boy whom you especially want to meet. Perhaps this friend might even arrange a blind date, and you might all go out together. A blind date is an acceptable way to meet a boy if you can trust the judgment of the girl or boy who is recommending the date.

If you begin your acquaintance with a boy by going out with another boy and girl, you may feel less shy. In any case, you learn to know boys only by taking advantage of opportunities to meet them. You cannot retreat into the excuse of shyness as a reason for not knowing boys. You overcome shyness as you learn, by practice, what to do in every situation.

Boy-crazy. It is natural and normal for high school girls to be interested in boys. You are not "boy-crazy" merely because you are interested in, and talk about, boys; you are more grown-up than the girl who has no interest in them or pretends to have none. Often, a girl who accuses you of being boy-crazy is doing it merely out of jealousy or to get a rise out of you. If you are going to show your interest in boys, you must, however, show it in ways which boys can accept. If a boy has walked home with you and carried your books, do not stand outside your house, laughing loudly, running your fingers through his hair, adjusting his necktie, kicking him in the shins, or pinching him. Some girls really do that and think that the boys enjoy it.

When a boy telephones, do not let him spend the evening in conversation with you. If he has so much to say, let him come to your home to say it. Besides, some other member of the family may need to use the phone. Never talk to a boy on the telephone unless he will tell you who he is. The chances are he is only trying to find out if you can be "kidded."

157

Telephoning a boy constantly is not only bad taste, it is poor technique. If you phone a boy too often, he begins to wonder whether you are "hard up" for dates. Besides, most boys prefer to do the calling themselves.

Actions which are too aggressive betray a girl's lack of self-confidence in associating with boys. If a girl wants to be popular with boys, she will learn to show her interest in them in subtle and effective ways.

Being Attractive

Two questions frequently asked by girls are: "What kind of girls do boys like?" and "How can I make boys notice me?" An important part of the answer to the last question is: Be attractive. This does not mean "pretty," dressed flashily, or made up conspicuously. Boys say they like best the kind of girl of whom they can be proud when seen in public, one who has a winning personality and a good disposition. They like a girl who does not sulk or become a "wet blanket" or try to act superior and give the impression of being better than everyone else at a party. They like a girl who can be depended upon to wear simple but chic clothes that are suited to her personally and right for the occasion. They like a girl to be well-groomed and to have good posture. They do not like a girl who is loud or crude at a party or at a dance, who tells questionable stories, or who sits with her legs apart or her feet up on the furniture.

The attractive girl is the girl who is at ease socially, who can talk well, and who can be gracious to everyone, even to a girl or boy whom she does not like. Such a girl probably also has a special skill or hobby, dances well, is good in

Boys like a lively and cheerful date. Learn to dance well, develop skill in sports and games, and join the fun.

sports, or perhaps plays a musical instrument. Because she is the kind of girl of whom the other boys approve, a boy's own self-confidence is built up by any attention that she gives to him.

159

How Many Boy Friends?

It is not wise to let one boy monopolize you. He may begin to feel sorry for you and to think that you cannot attract anyone else when he suddenly realizes that he is the only boy who dates you. This is part of the answer to the questions "How many boy friends shall I have?" and "Shall I have a 'steady'?" The other part of the answer is that you need to know many boys, in order to increase your knowledge of people and help you gradually to decide what kind of person you want to marry. You will be missing many opportunities for growing up if you hang on for dear life to the first boy whom you meet because you are afraid to meet other boys or afraid that you will never find another who likes you. Or are you assuming that the first boy you meet will develop into the perfect man?

While you are in high school, it is much to your advantage to go around with a group of boys and girls, so that your name does not become linked to that of one particular boy. If it is so linked, other boys may be afraid to date you, for fear that your "steady" will object. Then you are likely to lose a lot of fun, as well as interesting, friendly associations with other boys. If one boy does attempt to monopolize all your time, you might persuade some of your friends to go on double dates with you. Give yourself an opportunity to meet many different kinds of boys. Thus you help yourself to learn to be the kind of girl whom many boys finds attractive.

All this discussion presupposes that you are dating high school boys or boys a year or two older than you are. If, however, you are dating a man several years your senior, you have a right to expect that he is taking you out because he

160

enjoys being with you and likes you, that he will protect you and look after you. If this is not the case, if he will not come to your home and meet your family, if you must constantly be on your guard when you are with him, he does not deserve your company. Of course, no girl who has thought through the risks involved will ever go anywhere with a man she knows nothing about. Many men stop their cars to try to pick up girls. When girls accept invitations under such circumstances, men seldom feel that they are expected to act like gentlemen.

Entertaining Boys

You will find it most pleasant to meet and entertain boys at home, if that is possible. A boy always thinks more of you and is flattered if you ask him to call for you at home so that you may introduce him to your parents. You might suggest to your parents that you all remain together for a few minutes' conversation after he arrives. There is so much that you can learn about the boy as you see him in the company of adults: Can he carry on an intelligent conversation? How clever is he at finding something to talk about? What are his interests? Perhaps he will talk about school. His parents may know yours, or the two families may have friends in common. Do *your* part, also, to keep a short conversation going before your parents leave. Be interesting yourself, and draw out interesting conversation from the others. All this will help the boy to make a good impression on your parents.

If you know that the boy does not have much money, you can show real consideration by suggesting, at least occasionally, that you do things that do not cost anything—dance to records at home, play cards or games, or go out for a walk.

161

A date at home is fun, and it gives you an opportunity to learn about your boy friend's hobbies.

Above all, be careful that you do not ask the boy to spend too much money on you in one evening. If the evening's dance or movie has been expensive, try to arrange to bring him home for a bite to eat instead of eating out. If you are having your first date with him, plan to have your mother or another member of the family at the door to greet you both briefly when he brings you home. This will make him feel welcome and at ease in your home. He will also feel that he has been accepted by you and your family and will be much more likely to ask you for another date.

A problem that some girls have to face is lack of space in

their own homes for entertaining boys. What can you do then? In a number of communities teen-age centers are the answer to this problem. Most communities have some organization or social center where high school boys and girls are welcome. Another solution may be to plan with a friend for the two of you to give a party at her home. Again, some of your older friends may be happy to have you call on them.

Keeping a Boy's Friendship

After you have met a boy and have gained his friendship, the question "How can I keep his friendship?" inevitably follows. The answer is: See to it that the boy enjoys being with you. Are you the kind of girl of whom he can be proud? He knows something about you from the way you act in school. He learns more from your response to his first request for a date. If you wish to accept, but really have another date, are you considerate enough and wise enough to suggest another day? Remember that the boy may sometimes be more bashful than you are. A complete rebuff from you might discourage him from ever asking you again. Do not refuse him discourteously, even if you do not particularly like him. There is never an excuse for lack of courtesy. You may find that you like him better after you are better acquainted with him—and you may meet other boys and girls through him.

When you have your first date with him, plan, if possible, to do something at which you appear at your best. Do not go to a dance if you cannot dance well. However, if you are attending a party together, and you know that you will be expected to dance with the boy, turn on the radio or phonograph at home before you go. Dance first at home, so that you may become familiar with the steps that the boy uses

163

and with his method of dancing. If you play tennis well, you might suggest a game of tennis. If you play the piano, it may be possible to demonstrate this skill. Put yourself in a situation in which you feel at ease. Then you will appear at your best.

One of the necessities for building an enduring friendship is that you be natural at all times. Never pose or brag. Know, also, how to put a boy at ease. He may be embarrassed or even seem moody. Discover his interests and try to learn something about him. Girls should know about many things —sports, books, politics, what is going on in the world. As with your girl friends, do not be selfish. Be interested in the boy, not in yourself alone. Find out what his abilities are, and encourage him to develop them. Build up his self-confidence, whether it be in athletics, a hobby, or his school-work. Never act as if you knew everything. If you constantly argue with a boy, or question his opinions, you will usually make him feel inferior. Try to enjoy being with him, and act as if you did.

You need, in your associations with boys, to develop a sense of humor. This does not mean merely telling funny stories; it means keeping a sense of perspective. Know the important from the trivial; do not get angry at little things. Even though a boy may have taken you to a party and another girl "cut you out," it is unwise to show your feelings, to have tears or a scene on your way home. Ignore the incident, even though you may have decided never to accept another date with that particular boy, should he ask for one. On the other hand, do not pout or be jealous when a boy merely dances with another girl. If you know other people in a group, you probably will be exchanging dances with several couples during the evening.

If you want to keep a boy's friendship, the necessity of showing your appreciation of favors cannot be overemphasized. Never take the boy's courtesies for granted. If you are dancing with him, be courteous and appreciative. This does not mean that you need to warble, "Thank you," after each dance. Instead, compliment him on a trick step, for instance, to let him know that you are enjoying dancing with him. In addition, you can show your appreciation by devising ways to return his favors—such as having a party or planning a picnic for which you furnish the food.

What about Smoking?

A question often asked by high school girls is: "Shall I smoke when I'm out on a date with a boy?" Several years ago, smoking was considered smart—"the thing to do." Many girls were afraid of being labeled "slow" or "unsophisticated" if they admitted that they did not smoke or if they did not like smoking.

Now girls discuss smoking very casually. Many girls do not smoke because they do not care to do so. A taste for tobacco, like a taste for olives, is acquired; many girls simply do not like tobacco. They may have tried cigarettes and disliked their taste. Consequently, when a cigarette is offered them, they refuse it with a polite, "No, thank you—I don't care for any," just as they would refuse a meat or vegetable they dislike. On the other hand, if a girl wants to smoke, the consensus among high school girls seems to be, "I don't hold it against her so long as she doesn't make a point of the fact that she smokes. When she does that, she's just showing off." A girl should know when, where, and how to do it in good taste. High school girls are more interested in why girls smoke than in whether they smoke.

If a girl is so obvious about her smoking that she uses it as an attention-getting device, she needs to ask herself, "Why do I want to smoke?" If you reach for a cigarette at a party because you are ill at ease and do not know what to do with your hands, then you had better acquire, instead of smoking, the social ease that can displace that awkwardness. If smoking is an excuse to stay off the dance floor, then it is wiser to learn to dance well. If it is a substitute for having to keep up a conversation, learn to talk well. If you think that you must smoke because your crowd happens to do so, then ask yourself, "Do I intend to spend the rest of my life following others, sheep fashion?" If you smoke because your parents said that you should not smoke, see whether you cannot grow up past the point where you derive satisfaction from mere rebellion.

Stand on your own feet. If you do not want to smoke or if you do not enjoy it, merely say so. If you consider cigarettes a waste of money you prefer to use for a clothes budget, don't buy them. If you have decided that you do not wish to smoke until you are older, courteously refuse cigarettes when they are passed. Even if a boy offers you a cigarette when you are out on a date with him, you are under no obligation to accept. Remember, boys respect a girl who can make her own decisions. Another fact to consider, girls say, is that "lots of boys don't want you to," and "especially if a boy doesn't smoke, he doesn't seem to want you to smoke."

If a boy himself does not smoke, or if he is not accustomed to seeing his mother and sisters smoke, he may believe that women should not smoke. Boys often express this feeling with "It doesn't look well" or "I want my girl to act feminine." Smoking seems, to many boys, a masculine habit.

166

Moreover, a girl's smoking may embarrass the boy. By your smoking when he refrains, you place him in the category of someone who is immature while you, supposedly, are sophisticated. Every boy wants you to consider him not only grown-up but a "he-man."

Curiously enough, although many high school boys themselves smoke, they often do not like to see their girls smoke. Many a boy offers a girl a cigarette and, when she accepts it, says in a surprised tone, "*You* don't smoke." Thus, the girl may fall from the pedestal on which boys often place girls they like. Boys frequently want as a friend someone whom they can admire, almost adore. You may resent the pedestal type of admiration, although as a rule girls find it very pleasant to be adored and want to live up to the ideal.

There is also the fact that some girls have been told by doctors that they are growing fast, are nervous, and that, at present, it would be injurious to their health for them to smoke. This is common sense. Consider what happens to most boys and girls the first time they smoke. They seldom enjoy it; they often feel nauseated. Should you wonder why, the handkerchief test may give you the answer. If even one mouthful of smoke is blown through a handkerchief, it leaves a dark-colored deposit. This is evidence of the same tars which affect some people unpleasantly and are responsible for stained fingers, smelly clothes, and offensive breath.

Continued smoking affects different people in different ways. People who smoke only two or three cigarettes a day all their adult lives may use tobacco with few ill effects. However, excessive smoking may irritate the lining of the respiratory tract or cause an annoying cough or even more serious complications. All this may seem a long way off. Yet

167

many high school girls already have noticed that "some girls want a cigarette every time they turn around" or that "it gets to be a nervous habit." Smoking does develop a hold on some individuals, and it is obvious that the earlier one begins to smoke, the stronger the hold smoking may take.

Just what kind of hold do cigarettes have? Many of the high school girls who smoke do so because they think that it is the social thing to do, even though they dislike it. When a girl is new in a school and someone with whom she would like to become friendly offers her a cigarette, she may take it. Or, when she is unable to make conversation with a boy or is in a roomful of strangers, a cigarette seems to help. But smoking does not hide her social awkwardness; anyone can recognize when a cigarette is being smoked for effect. Are you going to continue throughout life lighting cigarettes to give yourself the illusion of having social poise, or are you going to develop the interest in other people that will make you a friend to be sought and an attractive girl to date? Nothing can give you sophistication, worldliness, or the ability to handle social situations with poise except experience in handling social situations, knowledge about yourself, and knowledge about other people.

What about Drinking?

The question of drinking is a serious one. You might begin by asking yourself why you want to do it. If your reasons are the same ones that you gave for smoking, apply the same tests to your answers. Understand, too, that the boy may be drinking for reasons similar to those you gave. He may be trying to appear grown-up. He may want to see if you will take a dare. Or he may have discovered that drinking gives him a feeling of self-confidence—makes him able to talk. In fact, you both may think that drinking is the way to make up for a feeling of inadequacy. It is a poor method, a refusal to face the real issue. It is like going to a party with your eyes bandaged.

Alcohol acts as a narcotic. It makes you say and do things that you ordinarily would not say and do—actually makes you a different person. Suppose you do want to be different. Is drinking the wise way to change yourself? Isn't it more grown-up to make yourself an attractive person, so that you will not need to change yourself by drinking? Moreover, there is an important health question to consider, one probably much more important than the health question in relation to smoking. You probably know that it is illegal, in most states, to sell liquor to anyone under eighteen. These laws were passed not because a few "crackpots" are opposed to liquor but because responsible citizens want to hand over this country to healthy young men and women.

Alcohol breaks down controls. It works this way: When it enters the digestive tract, it is absorbed without being changed by the digestive juices. The blood carries the alcohol to all parts of the body. The effect of the alcohol is most noticeable in the brain, where it dulls some of the nerve centers. It is this effect that produces the deceptive feeling of stimulation, the overconfidence that causes a person to become talkative, sociable, and boastful. Such behavior is the signal that judgment, will power, and self-control have been weakened. With continued drinking, speech becomes indistinct, because the next thing that happens is that the speech centers in the brain lose partial control of the vocal cords. Then the motor areas of the brain—

169

those having to do with muscular activity and coordination—lose partial control of the muscles, and staggering results. Finally, the sensory (those that enable us to receive sensations) and motor areas of the brain are so deadened that the person lapses into unconsciousness.

One group of high school girls implied their attitude toward drinking in this statement: "If a girl once sees another girl drunk, she'll never want to drink." They described a scene at which they had been spectators the week end before. "A girl was sitting near us in the restaurant with her boy friend. She was good-looking—so were her clothes. She had a cocktail in front of her. When we came in, we could hear her loudly telling her boy friend that this was her third and that she couldn't feel a thing. She said it over and over, with her voice getting louder all the time. The boy got terribly embarrassed—and so did we. Of course, he probably got her to take a drink in the first place, but now, you could see, he wished he hadn't. Men in the restaurant began to make cracks about her. She looked awful; her eyes were hard and glazed and her mouth was partly open. But she didn't realize it." No—she was probably conscious only of a feeling somewhat like relaxation—nothing seemed worth worrying about. Her shyness was gone. She was talkative, not because she was stimulated, but because her inhibitions were down. Her thick speech may have seemed cute to her; her words may have sounded far away. She talked continually louder in order to try to catch up with her voice. Her conversation may have seemed, to her, very funny. Certainly it included many things she would have considered indiscreet, things she would never have said if she were sober.

One of two things will result for this girl: She may overestimate the strength of her stomach and become violently ill. In that case not only will she suffer from severe nausea and dizziness, but she will also be very humiliated. This situation, however, is preferable to the alternative of developing a craving for alcohol. Along with the so-called "ability to consume large quantities of liquor without becoming ill" is a lessening of discrimination and a dulling of the senses which, the next morning, results in the bitter feeling that one has been somewhat cheap and silly, has said too much, has taken too many chances, or has gone too far. Obviously, drinking is related to petting. Drinking breaks down the controls—the will power and judgment which you would retain had liquor not dulled your consciousness of what you were doing. You are unfair to yourself when you allow such a situation to develop.

Why do people drink? Many people really don't like the taste of alcohol as well as that of ginger ale or other soft drinks. But a moderate amount of liquor, taken by adults in the company of other adults, has pleasant effects. It induces relaxation after a tense day. However, it cannot conjure up gaiety and high spirits for long. It is not a stimulant but a depressant. Its immediate effect on the brain has been noted: First, it acts as a sedative, because it relaxes one; then, in large quantities, it acts as an anesthetic and produces lack of inhibition and coordination.

This discussion does not presuppose that you should be grimly set against drinking for the remainder of your life. If your parents indulge in occasional cocktails, no one, not even doctors, will object. Doctors and psychologists will argue, however, that alcohol is a drug and, like any drug, is habit-forming. Some individuals may gradually develop such a

171

craving for alcohol that the craving dominates behavior to the extent that the individual lacks the judgment and self-control of a responsible citizen. Liquor is, for such a person, a dangerous form of self-indulgence. Naturally, comparatively few individuals who have occasional cocktails become alcoholics. But mature judgment is needed to decide when, where, and how much one can drink.

If, when you become an adult, you decide that you wish to drink and smoke occasionally, your judgment will have become trustworthy enough so that you know there is real satisfaction only in moderation. Meanwhile, you will have built habits and behavior patterns that have made it possible for you to grow up to be an attractive, responsible woman who has given her body, her mind, and her reputation every chance.

During the next few years, therefore, you want to develop the technique of saying "No" without seeming to be a poor sport or a "prude." If someone offers you a cocktail, don't raise your eyebrows and sneer, "No, I don't drink!" Or when cigarettes are passed, don't exclaim with a superior air, "I never touch tobacco!" Such an attitude is antisocial, impolite, and unnecessary. Merely smile and say, "No, thank you." Should anyone be bad-mannered enough to make fun of your tastes, merely explain matter-of-factly that you see no reason for taking something you really don't enjoy.

When you are out with a boy, the question of drinking may arise at a party or at an eating place after the party. At a party in a private home, or at a chaperoned fraternity or hotel dance, you may find that there is liquor in the punch. You may have graciously accepted punch. You may have taken a sip of it, but there is no necessity for drinking more.

172

Small tables or window sills are always available. Leave your glass without being obvious about it. You can also, in subtle ways, control your partner's drinking. Instead of giving him the opportunity to make a dash for the punch bowl during a dance intermission, find some excuse for him to take you out to eat. Solid food makes drinking less harmful.

It is possible to avoid placing yourself in an embarrassing position by refusing even to accept a date with a boy if you know that he drinks excessively. However, if a boy with whom you have come to a party does drink more than he should, by all means ask the parents of your hostess to see you home. At a hotel dance or a fraternity dance, go to the chaperon for advice, or call a taxi. If you haven't enough money, your parents will be glad to pay the fare when you arrive home safely. The host at the party will see that the boy gets home. Most of the time, however, the drinking question is in your control if you accept your responsibility. You are the guest of the boy; he will usually consider your wishes.

You can also, without being self-righteous or obvious, control the question of drinking after the dance. The boy generally asks you whether you wish to go out to eat. Suggest a place that does not serve drinks. The boy usually will not mind; hamburgers or sodas are cheaper than liquor. Or, if the dance was late and you are expected at home, suggest that you go home to eat. You might even have discovered his favorite food and be able to say, "Mom baked some angel cake today" or "I bought some hot dogs and mustard this afternoon." Especially if the dance was an expensive one, he will appreciate your thoughtfulness.

However, if you have allowed the boy to insist upon having a drink, you still can order a fruit drink or a coke or ginger ale for yourself and do it graciously, saying, "I'd rather have this." Say it naturally, not apologetically or in a superior manner. This situation, again, calls for social technique, a knowledge of what to say and how to say it. When you have both been served, you can control the boy's drinking by sipping your own drink. Make one drink last a long time. This presupposes that you are able to carry on a conversation that will interest the boy.

Do the same thing if you are at a restaurant with a group of boys and girls. Girls can usually control the boys' drinking, or they can order food and share it with the boys. When they can no longer carry the conversation, they can suggest that the party adjourn to the home of one of the girls. There is always at least one girl in the crowd who can count on her parents to be understanding in such a situation.

If, in spite of everything, your boy friend drinks too much, see that the boys take him home. Someone among the group will undoubtedly volunteer to take you home. If not, you can call a taxi or call your parents. Do not act shocked or create a scene, but do take care of yourself. Never expose yourself to the hazards of being accompanied by an irresponsible escort, either in a car or on a walk home. You may not wish to date the boy again, or you may feel that you can overlook one such occurrence. You will not want the incident to pass unnoticed, however, as though you did not care what he was or what he did. Discuss the situation with him before you go out again. Talk frankly and intelligently, but do not resort to humiliating or rudely taunting the boy.

If you have any reason to believe that a certain boy, given an opportunity, may become irresponsible in the matter of drinking, do not give him that opportunity. Inquire carefully about the evening's plans before you go out. Know what time the movie or dance that you are attending will end, and then have your parents set the hour when you are due at home in such a way that the boy has just time to get you home without any stopovers. In a situation as serious as that to which drinking can lead, you cannot take chances. If the boy is the kind of boy you like, he will appreciate your helping him not to drink. If he does not respect you for taking care of him and yourself, you will not wish to continue dating him. You certainly do not want to drive with a boy who has been drinking. An alarmingly high percentage of the most ghastly auto accidents are caused by drunken drivers. Many girls have been killed or crippled because they drove with boys who had been drinking. Adults are learning to refuse to ride with drunken drivers; they know the risks involved. For the sake of your own safety, you must learn never to take such risks.

The Boy You Like

Every high school girl is confronted with the question "How can I build up between myself and my boy friend a friendship that will be genuine, that will mean something to both of us, and that I can look back upon with satisfaction because it contributed to my growth, increased my self-confidence and my knowledge of people, and added to my happiness during my high school years?" You want to put your best thinking to work on this question. It is as important as any problem that you will face in a lifetime. Year by year, you will want to learn more and better answers to this question, for you can never shut boys and men out of your life without losing much that life has to offer you. You need the stimulus of their companionship, their points of view, their friendship.

A successful friendship is a give-and-take—a happy, meaningful relationship in which both of you are at ease. Such a friendship develops gradually as you and your boy friend learn to know and respect one another, as you discover that you like to talk together, to work together on committees in school, to skate, to read, to walk, to be in plays, to dance together, or to share other interests. Naturally, the time comes when you both want to show your appreciation of that friendship. At first, you do it in words. You smile and thank him for opening the car door, for holding your coat as you put it on. You compliment him for his choice of clothes—"I like your suit" or "That's a good-looking sweater"—or for his choice of friends. If you are returning from a party at the home of friends of his, you might say, "Your friends are fun. They made me feel at home almost as soon as we arrived." You comment on the skillful way in which he handles social situations—"Mother and Dad enjoyed talking to you. How did you find out so soon that Dad is crazy about flying?" Or, when you are attending a dance to which a friend invited you both, you might say, "It was nice of you to ask Jane's sister for a dance!" Thus you build up his confidence and self-respect; you help him to believe that he is a worthwhile person. All of us need such reassurance and encouragement.

Not only do you let a boy know by words that you like him. Your actions and your consideration of him are revealing. You graciously accept his invitations—"Yes, I'd like to go. Thank you for asking me." You do not take it for granted that on Saturday night he will provide entertainment for you. You are ready when he calls for you. When you are

176

Tell your date how much you have enjoyed the evening.

with him, you let him know that the evening is enjoyable—
"It's a good picture, isn't it?" or "I'm glad we came to the
party." You act as though you were proud of him; you introduce him to your friends; you create opportunities for him
to display to advantage whatever talents he has; you talk
with him as though his conversation really interested you.
Nothing more quickly blasts a friendship than a matter-of-

177

course attitude, rudeness, or a lack of sincerity. If you accept invitations and gifts as though they were your due, if you are bored or looking around for other conquests during a boy's conversation, if you leave your date for several dances because you have found a better dancer, or if you "hand him a line," no real friendship will develop.

What about Petting?

When a friendship has developed out of mutual understanding and consideration, it is natural that a boy and a girl feel and want to express affection for one another. You should, by all means, be affectionate. You become cold, hard, and selfish if you do not care deeply about other people. Of course, the expression of your friendship must be real. You must mean what you say and do.

This is the reason why the argument that you express affection with a boy or pet with him because he expects it breaks down. You are not fair, or even decent, to a boy if you are dishonest with him, if you pet because you want him to spend more money on you or because you are afraid that, if you refuse to pet, he will not ask you for another date. Affection cannot be demanded; what you express because you are expected to express something is pretense and leads both of you to disillusionment. Moreover, if a girl assumes that a boy intends to dominate her or to take advantage of her when she is not on her guard, she will be cautious and fearful, rather than natural and happy with boys.

When the question of petting arises, treat a boy like a human being, like someone whose friendship you value. Treat him as you'd want another girl to treat your favorite brother who means a great deal to you. A boy appreciates decency and fair play, frankness and sincerity, which assure him that you will say and do only what you believe. Let the boy know where you stand on the question of petting, but never lecture him in an embarrassed or self-righteous manner.

Be sure that the affection you express says to the boy what you mean to have it say. If a boy whom you respect and like kisses you good night, do you each understand what the kiss means to the other? Perhaps to you it is just "thank you," or, "I had a lovely evening," or, "good night." If it is, do you want to say that with a kiss? If you do, does the boy know that your kiss means only that, or does he think that it means, "I'll let you go this far tonight"?

After all, there are only a few ways in which you can express, in some physical manner, your affection for a boy. You do not want to use up these few ways all at once, or they will become playthings with no meaning. "Going through the motions" when you do not feel what you pretend to feel breeds bitterness for both you and the boy. If you make of something precious a cheap and shoddy thing, you condemn yourself to doubt that the real thing—genuine affection—exists, because you have known only imitations.

You want life to become richer as you grow older. The time will come when you will want to express real love, a deeper feeling than any affection you now know. You will want new ways of doing it. Therefore, you will choose carefully, out of the narrow range of ways given human beings of showing affection, the ways in which you will express the feelings you have now for the boys who are your friends. You will say, in your affection for those boys whose companionship you enjoy, only what you really believe—

179

that you like them, that you enjoy their company. The only valuable friendship is a mutual relationship. When you like each other and know that you have much to contribute to one another, you each take care of the other in order that each of you can trust the other to do his or her best to preserve the genuine quality of your friendship. If whatever you do or say is sincere, you will earn your companion's highest praise, that which a boy bestows on a girl when, in describing her, he says, "She's really swell."

Many girls cannot formulate any definite convictions about petting because they continually confuse it with love. Petting is only one part of love; it is its physical manifestation. Real love is not based on the physical, biological goal alone. Love is much more than that; it requires more maturity.

Love is a complex of human relations in which the physical, mental, emotional, and spiritual aspects are all necessary. To limit it to the expression of one aspect would be inadequate, even absurd and impossible. Love confined to the mental and spiritual plane is like a painting without color. A merely physical love on the sexual plane is disillusioning. The enjoyment of the physical aspect of love depends so much on the feeling expressed, that without the feeling there is little physical satisfaction. There may be negative pleasure, a relief from physical tension, but this is often followed by depression and disappointment unless the more genuine and durable elements of love are present to make the experience meaningful.

For any important and permanent relationship, such as the love of a man and a woman, there must be a slow and gradual culmination. All the various elements in this com-

180

plex relationship must be brought into line. In consciousness love may seem to appear in a flash—simple, unique, and unchangeable, but in experience it has to be worked out with much labor over a period of time. Consequently, no matter what side of love—the physical, the mental, or the spiritual—has happened to take the lead, it cannot be allowed to monopolize the relationship.

It is important to have this perspective, to understand what petting really is—a part of the normal sex behavior of human beings, one of the driving forces of life, but one that is meaningful only when it is dovetailed with, and understood in relationship to, other phases of our behavior. Each of us is born into this world with certain dominant wishes or purposes. The most important and the easiest to explain in our behavior is self-preservation. Second in importance is the desire to see that, when our life span has been run, there is another human being to take our place, so that the human race may go on. Of course, we are not aware of these purposes when we are born. Probably we are not really conscious of them as we grow up. None the less, we act in accordance with them.

A baby is, for the most part, interested only in herself, in being comfortable and happy. Soon, she becomes increasingly interested in her mother. This expanding interest gradually includes more and more members of her family. Then it includes her playmates. Next, she shows a preference for the company of members of her own sex. Finally, with the coming of physical maturity and the bodily changes which it involves, there comes a tendency to be interested in members of the opposite sex. The adult unites three interests: her interest in her own origin or in that of the race, her interest in her physical self, and her interest in another person. This triple emphasis is essential to a mature marriage in order that life in this world may go on.

This is the meaning of the drama of *falling in love*. Many of its manifestations you know. It is an interest in boys and in all that makes a girl attractive to them, an interest in love stories, a seeking for attention. A boy and a girl meet in a gathering of people. One sees in the other something that interests and attracts. This interest grows. Meetings are arranged. They enjoy one another's company. Then they may "fall in love."

The girl "in love" is happy and optimistic. The world looks bright. Her work seems easy. She may secure a great deal of satisfaction from giving her feelings expression in writing, from daydreaming, from reading prose or poetry expressing feelings which she recognizes, or from doing nice things for the boy whom she loves. When the boy is near, her heartbeat accelerates; she smiles; she feels joy at being in his presence. There is a desire for increasingly close, intimate association.

Such a romance may be stopped at any stage. But, left to itself, its development is in the direction designed by nature for the continuation of the race. The aim of every species in the natural world is to reproduce itself. Petting stimulates in both partners feelings and desires which may be hard to control. Continued petting may precipitate a desire for immediate gratification of a strong drive and may result in serious consequences.

This does not mean that an occasional kiss will lead into uncontrolled sex behavior. Girls need information about the way in which their bodies and feelings work if they are intelligently to think through their attitude toward kissing

182

and petting. They need also to be freed of misconceptions such as those revealed by a group of high school girls who expressed anxiety because their boy friends considered kissing a normal expression of affection, while they feared that pregnancy would result from kissing and embracing. A kiss on the cheek, a brief, friendly squeeze of the shoulders cannot be called petting. However, a prolonged kiss and caressing of the body do constitute petting, because their purpose is the stirring up of sex desire or passion.

Just what are the implications of petting? Petting stimulates, or starts off, in both boys and girls, a set of physical sensations. A girl feels a general uneasiness, a restlessness, an excitement, possibly a tightness in the throat, a tingling in the spine, a choking sensation caused by the heart pumping fast and necessitating faster breathing. She may not recognize these sensations as the stirring up of sex desire because she is not aware of the functioning of her sex organs as such. But it is important for her to know that this is the way her emotions and glands work, so that this vague feeling of discomfort can be recognized in its true significance. Since a girl's body is more slowly aroused physically than a boy's, she should control the situation. If she recognizes the difference in timing, in tempo of sexual desire between herself and the boy, she will not only exercise self-control, but she will also recognize her responsibility for not "leading a boy on."

The boy has, in general, the same physical sensations as the girl. Moreover, a boy grows up with less fear about sex and with more recognition of his own physical and sexual development. His sensations are more localized than a girl's, since his sex organs are located outside his body. He is very

183

much aware of the preparation of his body for the sex act. Prolonged kissing and petting a member of the opposite sex cause a rush of blood to the veins of the male sex organs. The boy's sex desires are aroused. Therefore, if a girl allows prolonged kissing and caressing, she is "leading him on." His self-control is threatened; he is driven by his own physical nature to desire more and more intimate contact. Then, as the girl suddenly decides to stop petting, the boy is left feeling tense, uncomfortable, and somehow defeated. On the other hand, should the girl allow the boy to persuade her to "go all the way," she faces severe consequences. Boys and girls need to know that this is the way their bodies and feelings work, so that they understand each other and can protect one another rather than fear one another or cause one another physical discomfort and risk.

A girl's response to a boy's expression of his affection has a great deal to do with his estimate of her. If you allow a boy to pet with you in order to bribe him to give you another date or because you want to make a conquest or because you are so eager to be popular with boys that you will do anything they suggest, boys will resent you, because no one respects a selfish, scheming individual. If you pet because "all the girls do it" or because you are afraid the boy will consider you stiff if you refuse or because you think it is smart, boys will despise you for the insincerity which they cannot help feeling. No one can, with impunity, use another individual to further his own ends. If you pet because you've run out of conversation or because you can't dance well or play games well, it is wiser to set about acquiring the accomplishments you lack rather than resorting to petting because you do not know how to do other things. The girl of

184

whom the boys say, "She can't dance and she can't talk and she won't walk, so what can I do but pet her?" is not the popular girl with boys; she is merely considered stupid. If you pet with a boy because you don't know how to stop him when he begins, you are being cruel to him. It is your responsibility to know enough about the way petting affects you both physically to know how to stop him. It is also your responsibility to make clear your position on petting. Boys will often say that they pet because they think girls expect it; they fear that they might be considered slow if they did not try at least to kiss you. A boy may even be trying to find out if you are the kind of girl who will let him get away with it. If a boy is just adventuring or trying to see how much of a man he is, his expression of affection will have little relationship to genuine affection for you. Should you allow him to do what he wants, it would have no meaning for you; for him, it would mean only something to tell the gang about tomorrow.

Boys are as confused on this question of petting as you are. They want you to like them and they want to show you that they like you. But they, just as you, do not quite know how to express their feelings; sometimes they may seem clumsy and awkward in what they say and do, just as you *feel* self-conscious and inept or inexperienced with them. Think of all the things that are on your mind when you are out with a boy: how your hair looks, whether you will be able to dance well with him, what you will find to talk about. The boy is as worried as you are. He is thinking, too: "Does she like the way I look, the way I act, or the way I dance?" He is wondering how he can prove to you that he is having a good time without getting into trouble with you. Is it surprising that some boys act "tough" or bold or silly in an attempt to cover up the fact that they do not really know what to say or do?

The kind of boy whom you want for a friend desires not so much that you pet with him as that you somehow give him the assurance that you want him as a friend. The important question is not "Shall I pet or shall I not pet?" but "How can I learn to express the fact that I like the boy?" The boy needs, as much as you do, the feeling that he is a worthwhile person. In the first part of this chapter, some ways in which you can give him this feeling were discussed. Most of all, let him know that you are the kind of girl who says and does only what she can honestly say and do. He wants to believe in you and he wants you to believe in him. He wants you to treat him like someone whose friendship you value, rather than like someone whom you can "use" or of whom you can take advantage.

It is important for you to learn how to build up another individual and how to get along happily with him without doing everything he asks. Specifically, you need to learn how to let a boy know, without being obvious about it, that you think he is "a neat guy, a swell fellow." You need to know how, without being boastful or self-conscious, to give and receive a compliment. Sometimes you want to know, without being rude, how to refuse a boy's invitation, how to get out of taking a cigarette, or how to avoid having to kiss or to be kissed. You need to know how to do these things in a friendly manner, without belittling the boy or being embarrassed or apologetic because you are afraid someone will consider you slow. Incidentally, those individuals who are most certain that they are popular and well liked by other

186

boys and girls are the ones least likely to feel that they must do what the gang does.

You need, also, to think ahead to social situations that may confront you and to possible ways of meeting them. When is the question of petting most likely to arise? You probably find it easy to decide that you do not care to advertise in public your affection for the boy. Therefore, you do not care to have a boy sit with his arm tightly around you in a public restaurant or with his head draped on your shoulder in a movie. But what about riding home after the party in the back seat of the car, or parking, or saying good night?

If you are to ride in a car with someone else, you and the other girls can talk over the situation before the party and decide that you will have something to talk about with the boys—something that interests them, not just who wore what. You will not allow the boys to drive into the country, and you will leave the party just in time to get home at the hour you are expected with no stopovers on the way. If you are alone in a car with a boy, be sure that you know where he is going, that you know what to talk about with him, and that you have an answer, after the movies, when he wants to "drive around." You can always be hungry and have him take you somewhere to eat; then leave for home just in time to get there at the hour you are expected.

When you arrive home, express to the boy your appreciation of the good time you had. If one of your parents should be around, consider the parent not as a chaperon but as an audience for your recital of your good time. Suppose, however, that you think you owe the boy a kiss for numerous good times. One girl says, "I try to see that he has a good time throughout the evening. Then I don't owe him any-

187

thing." Another argues, "Kissing is all right, but I'm not interested beyond that." Make this clear to the boy. As one girl said, "Give him an ordinary kiss. It should have just enough affection in it to let him know that you like him, but not enough to be a 'come on.' Don't get starry-eyed."

If, in spite of your subtle discouragement of his caresses, a boy's hands roam, he is probably just adventuring, and you can call his bluff. That does not mean laugh it off, slap his hand, scratch his face, or inquire with a cold, fishy stare, "Do you have to do that to have a good time?" You can casually, but firmly, take his hand and put it back in his lap as you continue talking to him, or you can say in a friendly way, "Not so fast," or make some other remark that conveys your meaning clearly, but carries no censure. Meet the situation without humiliating or hurting the boy, without making him feel that you consider his actions "dirty" or "disgusting." Give him credit for decent motives; assume that he is trying to let you know that he likes you. We always want people to think the best of us. The kind of boy you want to date will respect your wishes and appreciate your tact. He will understand that you are differentiating between his actions and him and that you can discourage his actions, yet encourage him to continue to be friends with you.

Some girls, then, may drift into petting because of these reasons: They think it is expected of them; they want to be popular; they get a thrill out of it; they want to see what it is like. They discover that continued petting means facing the question "Shall I go all the way?" High school girls answer this question with realism and idealism—with an idealism that would astound adult cynics. Here is what they say:

"I believe in marriage; I want to keep that for my husband."

"That is an adult experience."

"I don't want to do that until I do it with a man I know I really love, and I don't know that yet."

"That's one privilege I want to reserve for a man I want to be really close to all my life."

"I'll kiss boys now if I like them, but I want something left for my marriage."

"I connect that with marriage; it wouldn't feel right now."

"I couldn't live with myself after it was over."

"I'd feel like a heel when afterward I found a man I really loved and had to tell him—and I'd want to tell him."

The parents of girls who say these things can go back to sleep when they awaken at midnight and find that their daughters have not yet returned from the movies.

Girls who have principles like these need no hysterical admonitions to refrain from the temptations of sex; they are armed with something stronger and more positive than fear. They are waiting for love; they want to keep their spiritual and bodily integrity for their husbands and children. They know that sexual intercourse always implies some choice of a sexual partner, and that it is always accompanied by deep inner consequences in the souls and bodies of both partners. Mating is always its aim; its end is another life, and it matters greatly to these girls what sort of fathers their children have.

Nor do girls fool themselves: "Oh, it's not easy to refuse, especially if you like the boy a lot. But you can't just think of your own pleasure at the time." These girls are not the spineless sort who give up when faced with difficulties. They know that all the valuable things in life require self-discipline. Nor are they selfish; they know that every privilege carries a responsibility and that, throughout life, the rights of others must be considered. Moreover, they recognize what fear and lack of self-respect can do to a girl. They say:

"It's awful to have a bad reputation."

"I'd hate myself for being a girl who is 'easy to get.'"

"I'd always wonder whether I was all right, for the boy who goes in for that might carry germs."

"People say you're safe, but there's always a chance! Too many girls have gotten pregnant when they didn't intend to. I'd hate to be scared all the time."

"After a while, a girl who did that would be lonely."

"Nice fellows would hear stories about you and wouldn't date you."

"Fellows don't really respect a girl like that. They may take her out for a good time, but they're not proud of her and wouldn't want to marry her."

"I feel sorry for a girl like that. I think sometimes girls just let themselves in for that because they don't know about sex. Sometimes it's because they're not sure of themselves and are afraid they'll lose the boy if they don't do it."

"Your friends wouldn't think much of you, and you've got to have friends."

These girls know the strength of the standards about sex behavior demanded by society. One group of them said: "We made lists in social studies the other day. The boys put down what they expect in a girl they want to marry, and the girls did the same for what they expect in a boy. At the top of every one of the boys' lists was *sexual purity*."

"After all," said one of the girls, "it makes sense. I wouldn't want a child to grow up without a father."

190

These same girls discussed the fact that "you might marry the boy later," but they decided that "you'd always wonder whether he really respected you, and he might always wonder whether you'd do it again with somebody else. After all, you took a chance once."

"And," one girl said, "it would be awful to live with a man and know he couldn't trust you."

The girls summarized with, "I think it comes down to this: Do you want to be popular with boys because you're good fun and have a nice personality or because they can get you?"

The fact that you decide not to go in for indiscriminate petting with any boy should not mean that you are afraid to let boys touch you. Be friendly with them; show them that you enjoy being with them; and see to it that they enjoy being with you. Have fun with them; know how to do many things with them; and do not resent their impulsive embraces. Don't draw away with that shocked, "Young man, what are you doing?" look in your eye if a boy squeezes your arm. If you like the boy and you are glad that he likes you, let him know that. Respond with a natural, pleasant, and appreciative smile to the expression of affection of the boy whom you genuinely like. Such a response does not mean that you are issuing an invitation for further action. Sometimes, girls are so afraid of being thought fast, so eager to be considered good girls, that they make a scene and humiliate a boy over trivialities. Or they think that they can hold a boy's interest by pretending to be cold to any attentions. They may even have the unfortunate idea that physical contact of any kind is somehow "wrong."

If you can see petting as only one part of love, if you can enjoy the presence of boys and not be afraid of some physical contact, then you are the companion whom boys will seek and admire. You are the girl who is growing up because you know that you can learn to love only by loving, and that does not happen in a vacuum. You are having a succession of opportunities to know how to make friends with boys. You are learning to know many boys so that you may grow up a step at a time into the kind of woman who will finally be capable of mature loving and who will be able to contribute her proper share in the creation of a happy marriage and a happy home life with her husband and her children.

Is It Love?

What is real love? This question comes into the mind of every girl at some time or another. Most of the time the deepest kind of love experience does not come to the high school girl. She has not associated enough with boys; she does not know enough about any one boy. Each one whom she meets may seem to be better than the last; yet, while she is with him, she may see another with whom she thinks she would like to become acquainted.

What, then, are some of the qualities of mature love? Mature love for a husband is compounded of two feelings: One of them is mutual attractiveness on a physical basis. You must feel this deeply for a man you love. However, physical attraction must be combined with another feeling—the kind of feeling that you have about people who mean a great deal to you in life—the feeling that they are marvelous people. You may recognize their faults, but this does not mean that you care any less for them or respect them less. Another evidence of a mature woman's love for her husband is that she wants him as the father of her children. She sees a man as a wonderful father. Few high school girls can imagine that of the boys whom they know.

You must feel all this about the man whom you want to marry, if your marriage is to be happy and lasting. You must be able to express your love in all that you say, in all that you are, in all that you do. Love needs expression.

But expression must be learned. Love's requests cannot be made or answered in words alone. Just as mere talk cannot convey the meaning of a piece of music or a beautiful poem, no verbal declaration of love can come anywhere near to expressing what the lover wants to say. He must feel it and learn to say it by acts, by gestures, by the entire language of life and of art. Even physical expression of love is only a small part of love. Are you able to be a stimulating companion, a true friend, an understanding listener, an appreciative recipient of your partner's love? You can show your love for the man you marry by keeping your home lovely, by sewing on his buttons, by sharing his business anxieties, by remembering to do the favors he asks of you. If you feel that you can, in ways such as these, share many aspects of life with your future husband, you are learning to combine the spiritual and physical aspects of love.

You must be an adult emotionally as well as physically before you are, or can be, in love. Some people spoil a happy marriage relationship by their own fears, their own insecurity, their own selfishness. Perhaps they try to make over the person they love into their servant, into a copy of themselves, or into some unreal image that they hold. Perhaps they are afraid of love because they fear that a marriage relationship means giving up their own individuality, placing themselves in someone else's power. Perhaps they are unable to give themselves wholly to another because part of their love still remains at one of the baby levels, with Mother or Father or with themselves. They may even blight and blacken their happiness by jealousy, which is really an admission of their own inferiority, of their own cowardice and conceit.

A mature concept of love implies your understanding of the paradox that love seeks union, yet can exist only where there is freedom. If you love someone very much, you want to be with that person; you feel that, with him, you can be a different and better person than what you are alone. This is true. Not only in connection with the creation of a new being, but also through one another, two people in love can become a new being greater than either could be alone.

However, loving a person and living with a person do not mean that you attempt to possess or allow yourself to be possessed by that person. If two people do this, they destroy one another; they have nothing to contribute to each other. It takes maturity to love a person so much that you can become a part of his life, yet remain an individual and want him to remain so. More and more the mark of mature love is that unswerving refusal to "cage" another person, or to accept affection not freely and spontaneously given. In real love, there is no thought of fear or domination. Love does not mean that you place yourself in someone else's power. The only genuine power that one person can have over another is that power which is developed in you because of a growing feeling that you must be worthwhile since that person loves you. To give and to receive such love is doubtless the most difficult lesson human beings must learn. Not until we cease to be children emotionally can we learn it.

194

As you trust another person enough to love him, enough to place your life in his hands, as you give him the power to hurt you, you lose yourself in your concern about someone else. Thus you are freed of yourself; you are learning unselfishness. Because genuine love is more than personal happiness, love can show you the way to real freedom, the freedom that comes when you voluntarily tie up your life with that of another. Love can make you grow up. When you have grown to this mature concept of love, you will know the deep happiness which gives greatness to life. Unselfish love alone can do this. Such love then reaches out to others. It makes you see all of life in terms of unselfishness. It makes you want to share your joy with others, not because you think that you should, but because you have discovered what pure joy human life can be.

At first, this joy finds its expression in marriage; later, in the work that you and your husband do together to make a home. With love as its basis, work is glorified. You become more gentle toward others because you are happy. You want to unlock the doors of other lives that they, too, may know the peace, the freedom, and the glory that you have found in life. Your life is given purpose and justification. Sara Teasdale said, "I will sow my love so wide you will find it everywhere." This is what real love will mean to you. You will see beauty in life where you never noticed it before—in a lovely poem, in the sacrifice of a mother for her child, in the love of friend for friend, in the admiration of someone else for the person you love. You will resent ugliness of which you were not previously conscious, and you will want to help others to find a happiness approaching your own.

When you can know love like this, your life has been made

whole. Real love, however, will bring sorrow and pain, as well as the deepest joy. Into the development of a perfect alliance between a woman and a man must go infinite labor and patience, even pain and suffering. You may think that, by some lucky stroke and without effort, two people marry and live together happily, but all experience shows that this is not so. As in all the arts, so in the art of living together, no lasting result is attained without labor, suffering, and pain. Sacrifice, understanding, sympathy, and tolerance of the person one lives with are unalterable conditions of any genuine and permanent alliance.

You must be prepared to face disappointment, disillusionment, misunderstanding, separation, possibly even death, in your relationship with a man whom you love with a mature love. You may shrink from love like this because you are afraid of the future, because you cannot bear to face suffering. You must suffer in order to learn to be kind. Wisdom such as this can come only when you yourself have known life's pain as well as its joy. If you never deign to suffer, you can never understand another's sorrow or pain; you have no depth of feeling; you may become hard as well as shallow. These labors and sufferings are worthwhile, for out of them the souls of human beings are formed and carved into fitness for each other.

Therefore, live life as it comes. Take the hand of love when it is extended to you, and have no qualms or fears because you may be hurt. Of course, you cannot know the future of your love, but you do know that love is good and that the experience of loving and of being loved will enrich your life and will make you a finer person.

Early Marriage

Why do some teen-agers feel that they must marry so soon? Some blithely assume that everyone must marry. Since everyone's doing it, I must join the procession—or I might be left out. Girls have not always felt this way. Fifty years ago, almost a fifth of American women never married. Now about 6 per cent of sixteen-year-old girls and 25 per cent of eighteen-year-old girls are married. However, as our marriage rate has risen, so has our divorce rate, now one of the highest in the Western world. One explanation of this, no doubt, is that many a teen-age marriage has an unendurably thin foundation for lifetime happiness.

Why this rush to marry? The pressure begins early; in some *junior* high schools, boys and girls pair off because this practice is considered a sign of social success. In high school, some girls think they must snap up anyone available lest all marriageable timber for their age group be taken. After World War II, our new affluence, combined with our knowledge that one bomb might at any time wipe out life on earth, somehow precipitated in young people desires to "get what we want while we can." Parents who preferred to have daughter "settled down rather than worry nightly when she's coming in" applauded early marriages. Girls who wanted "careers" first were reassured that marriage need not interfere; indeed, it would help them to be "well-rounded" and therefore more creative in their jobs, better citizens, and better friends. Actually, this pressure to marry resulted in girls downgrading themselves as people and valuing themselves exclusively in terms of their marital rating. This attitude negates what

197

we know about growth. Girls should be encouraged in a serious concern with learning and in the development of their potentialities; from these experiences will come the wisdom, maturity, and stability that many early marriages lack. Moreover, education is important today not only because it has a bearing on a girl's ability to contribute to the family income, but also because—studies have shown—a girl's greatest asset in terms of her future children's development and well-being is the amount of education she has.

Pressure to marry is also the explanation of "going steady." Going steady is usually the girl's idea, although some boys embrace it because it is cheaper than spending money to impress a new girl each night or because they are bashful and would rather sit at a girl's house than go to parties. Many boys don't like it because, they say, a girl "gets to acting as though I were her property. She wants to know where I am every minute." Girls, on the other hand, usually go steady for social security. They want to know they'll have dates for important dances and "not end up with some creep," or they are "in love" with the boys and want to spend all their time with them.

The major hazards from going steady are implied in these stated reasons. The girl who clings to one boy does not meet, talk to, and get along with many kinds of people; she does not know how to have fun with people; she has a one-dimensional personality. The girl who is "in love" may find that the "dreamy" boy has become a habit with her; she begins to take him for granted. Statistics show that most "early marrieds" began dating at thirteen, going steady at fifteen, and at seventeen marry, often because going steady suggests that you "belong" to each other and "belonging" implies sexual privileges. It doesn't happen only to dumb boys and cheap girls!

Do these marriages work out? Of all divorces, 46 per cent involve girls who marry in their teens, and 74 per cent of all divorces involve those who marry under twenty-five. Conversely, 85 per cent of Americans who marry at twenty-five or over stay married. Why is this? Many teen-age girls never actually *choose* marriage; they are forced into it or they drift into it. "Everyone sort of expected us to marry," confessed a nineteen-year-old boy who had gone steady since he was barely fifteen. "I got tired of Sue even before I married her, but I had gone so far with her that I couldn't let her down." Unless one partner has the courage and skill to terminate a relationship like this before marriage, too frequently the divorce courts do so afterward!

Perhaps you are thinking, "If I get into a bad marriage, it's best to get out." No matter how logical this seems, if your marriage breaks up, in some sense you will always regret it. You are always hurt more deeply than you care to admit. Everyone comes out of a divorce with a sense of having failed in an important area of human relationships.

Loss of interest—by the boy for the girl or by the girl for the boy—is the greatest pitfall in early marriages. Lack of money is another. In fact, even when marriages are postponed beyond the teens, money becomes a major source of difficulty if the husband does not contribute to the family income. Yet in these days, education and training are a necessity. If a boy is eventually to earn a good living, college or advanced technical training is usually needed. Many a couple begin marriage agreeing that the bride will work to support both while the husband finishes his job training or college. They also may ask one or both sets of parents for help.

In these arrangements, however, there are hazards to a relationship. A married man, sponging on your mother—or his —for support, often feels that he is playing house at someone else's expense. Money has a peculiar significance in our culture. Men judge themselves harshly—and are judged harshly —if they fall short of what is expected of them in earning and spending. There is an edge in jokes like "Some parents not only send their daughter through college, but also her husband, dog, baby and baby-sitter!"

The couple soon learns that the wife's paycheck stretches only so far. If the girl dropped out of high school upon marrying, she has limited earning skill and must take any job she can get. In circumstances like these, even the gift of a new dress from concerned parents may complicate matters. The boy becomes angry because he thinks the parents are critical of him for not taking care of their daughter. Actually, he feels guilty about not contributing to the family income.

On the other hand, a girl may have had job training and may have a skill to sell. Yet often she may take "just any job" for its immediate advantages: it pays well and the hours coincide with the boy's studies "so we can at least be home together even though we hardly speak to each other—he's always studying." At first, a girl may think that she is willing to spend months, even years, at such a stop-gap job. But does this really happen? Will she, after a few months, resent having to negate her skills and interests and educational needs for her husband's? Or will she begin to feel that she too must prepare for her future if she is to be an individual as well as a wife? She probably *wants* to be a wife first and is willing to work at it. But is this enough? Each partner in a marriage needs other satisfactions—a meaningful job, a challenging

200

hobby, or opportunity for further study. Each must have something to contribute to a mutual relationship.

How does such a couple manage? Some decide the girl should take the challenging job for which she is prepared, even though it means less money. Some decide that the boy will work part-time, though it prolongs his preparation, so the girl can continue her education or develop her interests. Some couples cannot manage. The girl finds that she "can't take" the emotional strain of marriage when she has most of the responsibility. She "can't bear" rushing out each morning to a dreary job, while her husband "is at home reading a book." This same girl may have rushed into marriage shouting "I'm in love"— as though this were a magic formula to guarantee a future without problems!

The large amount of time the boy must spend studying also can be a source of quarrels. When the girl comes home from work, she wants to go out and have fun. But they haven't money to go out to dinner, so she cooks it. They haven't time to go out for fun; the boy has an exam next day. This is a realistic picture of many teen-age marriages. And we haven't considered what happens if a baby arrives, unplanned for! Have you?

Some teen-agers face and resolve these problems. They go into marriage with their eyes open. More mature than romantic, they learn how to live for the future. Chronological age has little to do with the understanding of the emotional— even financial—hazards involved in a marriage relationship. Are you ready for such a marriage? Whether you are sixteen or eighteen or twenty-one years old, only you can answer.

CHAPTER EIGHT

Deciding About a Job

WORK OCCUPIES an important place in the life of every individual. A job can give a girl a feeling of independence. It can teach her what is happening in the world. It can help her to see what her place in the world might be. Her work can furnish her with still another opportunity to learn how to get along with people. It can add to her self-confidence because, through her work, she often discovers new skills and abilities. In addition, in doing her job well, she finds an outlet for her energy and emotion.

Is a Job Necessary?

Naturally, most girls look forward to marriage, but marriage does not necessarily settle the problem of a job. Only the girl who has not grown up emotionally thinks of marriage as a way of being protected, taken care of, and waited upon. Today, women often work to supplement the family income. Whether married or not, a girl needs to have something to do that will give her real satisfaction. She may plan to continue her career after her marriage; she may develop a hobby to the point that her skill is recognized and appreciated by other people; she may assume responsible positions of service to the community. A woman with broad interests is not likely to become the kind of woman who needs to dominate her children's lives because she has no other outlet for her energies, nor will she feel, when her children grow up and leave home, that there is nothing left in life for her.

What Kind of Job?

The question of how to choose a job and how soon to secure one depends upon many factors. The decision will be quite different for the girl whose family can furnish her with whatever training she may need and for the girl whose earnings must be added, as soon as possible, to the family income. A girl's decision about a job will be influenced by the kind of ability she has, as revealed by the skills she develops, by what she likes or dislikes doing, and by the subjects she enjoys or dislikes in school. The selection of a job often depends upon whether a girl prefers to work chiefly with people or chiefly with things. Again, her selection may be determined by the motives that primarily influence her life. She may desire above everything else to be of service in the world, she may have a keen sense of religious duty, she may desire a job that will give her social prestige, or she may want one in which she can earn the largest possible amount of money in the shortest possible time.

A girl's choice of a job will be influenced also by factors over which she has no control at all, such as periods of national prosperity or depression, or the presence or absence of discrimination against her because of racial or national background. In the last analysis, the job that many girls finally

203

secure is determined by the type of work available in the community where they live. You may be surprised to know that statistics show that most girls remain near home. The greater the variety of work open to a girl, the easier it will be for her to secure the kind of work that she wants to do.

If it is at all possible, plan to do something which you will enjoy doing and in which you will have a reasonable chance for success. What that will be is influenced, of course, by your idea of success. If your ideal is money-making, you will choose whatever assures you the largest salary. If it is social prestige, you might do as some girls do—go into a certain kind of work, not because they like the work particularly, but because they think that through it they may meet people of superior social status. You may go to college, though you have no particular interest in doing so, because you think that a college education will help you to secure a better job.

Your standard of success may be set by your family's expectations of you. If your mother always wanted to be an interior decorator, she may decide to have you become one, whether or not you have talent for such work. Your father may have been limited in his choice of work because of a lack of formal education, and for that reason he may wish you to follow a profession. He may hope that you will be a doctor or a teacher, in spite of the fact that you do not feel yourself suited to work in the professions. Or, it may be that your father earned his way through college, got himself a good job, and "worked his way up" and that he thinks you should do the same thing.

These are some of the considerations governing your plans for your future. Other circumstances are present, but they are not the determining factors that they were once considered to be. For example, the idea is being overcome that women are somehow inferior to men and, therefore, must be excluded from certain positions. There are few occupations now in which women do not, or could not, have some part. It is evident, also, that outstanding mental ability alone does not assure success in a vocation. Studies of intelligence tests have proved that, though some kinds of ability can be measured, the *range* of ability cannot be determined, and it is one's range of ability that most often determines one's success in a job. A girl who consistently tops her class in schoolwork will not necessarily become a brilliant executive. For such work, in addition to academic ability, a girl needs capacity for taking initiative, ability in getting along well with people, and skill in making a good personal appearance. Aptitude tests and interest tests help to determine potentialities in these areas.

Discovering Yourself

How can you discover in what type of occupation you might have a reasonable chance of success? You can begin by knowing yourself, by seeing your interests, abilities, and accomplishments in relation to the need for them in society. Finding out what you can do that society needs to have done is important—far more important than either selfish desires or parental ambitions. Have you the outstanding sense of color, rhythm, and perspective which make up the equipment of an artist? Then develop this talent. Are you the kind of person who has to see how everything works, who minutely examines the household laborsaving devices or the inside of the family car, who loves any kind of machine, or anything

205

that she can do with her hands? Then a wide variety of possibilities is open to you in business and trades. You might enjoy operating one of the various types of business or industrial machines. You might become a technician or research person in a laboratory or in the communications fields. Home economics presents a constantly widening area of possibilities such as clothing and textile designing, nutrition, or demonstration of recipes and household appliances in stores or on television.

Are you frequently elected to class or club offices? Perhaps this means that you have the initiative and ability to secure the cooperation of other people, that you like to work with people. Teaching, nursing, social service, personnel work, merchandising, politics—all these you might well investigate and consider in relation to your own interests and capacities.

Do you gain your keenest satisfaction from pursuing a new idea, from working alone without interruption to develop the idea, whether in words, in a chemical formula, or in a mathematical equation? If your strong point lies here, you may become interested in scientific or mathematical research, writing, drawing, designing, architecture, or archeology.

There are other considerations, however, that will determine the degree of your success in a vocation, no matter what your chosen field. What sort of person are you? Do you generally act in a mature way, or do you frequently resort to infantile methods of behaving? Are you generally happy in working with people? Do you feel that they like you? You can discover something further about yourself by watching to see how well you get along with people at home and at school, by noting the kinds of courses which you enjoy, the household tasks for which you like to take responsibility, the types of extracurricular activities in which you engage, the skills or accomplishments in which you indulge in your leisure time. A great deal can be revealed to you about your own temperament as you observe your attitude toward your household or school tasks. Can you assume responsibility for them on your own initiative, or do you prefer to be told what to do? Can you be depended upon to get your work done on time, to remain at it until you finish, or must someone check up on you? Do you learn easily to perform a new task, or do you prefer to do the same thing over in the same way? Do you take pride in whatever you are doing, do it well, and not let anything interfere with your doing it? Do you have a good time at your work? The degree to which you do your work efficiently and well now is a fair indication of the way in which you can be depended upon to do it in an actual job later.

Whatever your temperament, ability, and accomplishments, the important consideration in making an intelligent choice of a vocation is that you face your ability realistically. Then ask yourself where in society this particular ability can be most useful. Next, begin your preparation for the vocation of your choice.

Seeking Advice

It is at this point that you most need wise guidance. Make the widest possible use of whatever facilities are offered you in your family, your school, your library, or your community for making a study of the occupational field in which you are interested.

Take advantage of whatever opportunities your school and

community give you to learn more. If a course in careers or occupations is taught in your school, enroll in it. If there is a vocational advisor, a counselor, a teacher, or a club leader in the school who will discuss your vocational problems with you, go to this person. Share freely whatever you may know of your own abilities, interests, and accomplishments in order that your advisor may have as much information as possible upon which to base his or her advice. If this person suggests that you take one or more of the various interest or aptitude tests used in vocational guidance, cooperate to the best of your ability in answering the questions. Although no tests are made that can tell all about you, a test can often be helpful in supplying additional information.

Ask your adviser to suggest courses that will serve as some part of your preparation for a job. Secure a list of books available in your school or public library concerning the occupations in which you are interested. You might compile your own occupations notebook. Such a notebook might contain material that you gather in connection with your reading or from your work at school, and newspaper or magazine clippings which you save because they include valuable items of information concerning occupations in which you are interested, such as graphs showing the trend of employment in these fields of work. In ways such as these you build up information about the training required, the conditions of work, the remuneration, the range of opportunities within an occupational field, the possibility of advancement, the advantages and disadvantages of the work, and the future of the occupational field.

When you have accumulated for yourself varied information about an occupational field and some pertinent questions about it are beginning to occur to you, it is wise to arrange interviews with some people who are engaged in this occupational field or to go where you can see people who are doing this kind of work in action. People are generally glad to talk with you about their work if you have definite and intelligent questions to ask them. They may be willing to conduct you through the manufacturing plant, the hospital, the insurance company, or the department store in which they work. Be careful, however, that you are not too easily influenced by their enthusiasm for their vocation; do not let them "sell you" a vocation because you like *them*.

Trying Yourself Out

You can learn even more about your abilities and limitations in reference to a particular occupation if you can secure a part-time job, after school or during vacation periods, in the occupation that seems interesting to you. Experience in an actual job will give you information about yourself that you could never get in another way. You will gain an idea of what an employer is likely to expect. You will discover the importance of getting to work on time, even when you have a headache, and of trying to be just as efficient as though you felt well. You will find that you must work even though the job to be done does conflict with a football game, a special matinee, or some other function that you hoped to attend. You will realize that your employer expects you to follow instructions the first time they are given, and that if a job has to be done, you do it, whether you like or dislike the piece of work.

You learn other things about holding a job, too. You find that it makes you feel very useful and independent to be earning your own money. You need the security of your home, but you need also to make a place for yourself in the world. You find out that, on a job, you will make good or fail according to your own ability and efficiency—that no one will praise or pay you unless you deserve it. You discover a great deal about people, too, by having to work with them, by being forced to figure out ways of getting along with them. Altogether, you begin to have quite a feeling of satisfaction, of being grown-up, and of knowing something about the world.

However, one word of warning here! You may be the kind of girl who is growing, or who has grown, so fast that you have a very limited supply of energy. This frequently happens to a high school girl. Then it would not be wise for you to run the risk of doing too many things. Your schoolwork and your health are most important now. However, if you have surplus energy and can never find enough to do at home to keep you busy, if you want more spending money, or if you are curious to find out, for instance, whether you would make a good nursery school teacher, then go over and take care of the neighbor's baby or become counselor at a children's camp or instructor at the community playground next summer. If you think retailing or nursing interest you, get a part-time job at the local dime store or be a nurse's aide at the hospital. Try yourself out at the kind of work in which you think you are interested.

On the basis of as intelligent a study of an occupation as you can make with all the resources available to you, decide upon some field for your lifework. Be certain that this decision about your vocation is yours rather than that of your parents or someone else whom you admire. Nor should your decision be the result of stories that you read, movies which

Part-time jobs and volunteer work provide opportunities for you to explore vocational possibilities and to discover your real interests.

you have seen, daydreams that you had as a child, or a desire to do what the crowd is doing. It is especially difficult to make and hold to your own decision if you must do it in spite of the disapproval of people whom you like.

You must have the stamina and confidence to hold to whatever decision *you* have made, if you are certain that it was made wisely. You must, at the same time, however, grant that other people also have a right to *their* opinions. Therefore, you give their advice careful consideration.

After you have made your choice and have your first job, your vocational problem is not necessarily solved once and for all time. You may have many changes ahead of you. Your job may not prove suited to your abilities. Moreover, occupational trends in employment show not only that the social and economic status of various occupations is changing rapidly, but that some occupations are actually disappearing, others are becoming overcrowded, while still others, scarcely recognized ten years ago as career possibilities, are growing increasingly important. No one can, with any certainty, predict the future of any one occupational field. By wise planning, however, it is possible to reduce the negative impact on you of these changes in the occupational world. Be willing to retrain for new jobs and to go where job openings are—even if this means leaving home. Be flexible in adapting your potentialities to new opportunities.

Be realistic about the number of job openings in a given field. For example, it is unwise for too many boys and girls to try to get into professions which statistics show can absorb only a small percentage of those seeking employment. Yet more than half the boys and girls in high school say that they are planning to enter a profession! Although there is a constantly growing need for social workers, doctors, nurses, and teachers, nevertheless, professional people are still a minority among workers in our country. It would be, therefore, short-sighted to build up one's conception of success around professional work or a white-collar job alone, as though these were the only areas in which enjoyment, satisfaction, remuneration, and an opportunity for service could possibly be found.

Applying for a Job

Next comes the question of securing a position. You must actively seek it. Staying at home—because you are embarrassed at the thought of "selling" yourself, frightened at the idea of competing with other applicants, humiliated at the thought of being "turned down"—merely compounds your fears. Begin your job-hunting campaign months before you need to go to work. Organize it intelligently. Use many tested methods, not just one. Seek the help of friends, relatives, school faculty members, and placement officers. Visit public and private employment agencies, and answer advertisements by letter and by making direct application. Keep adding to your list of names of people to interview, keep following new leads, keep writing letters and answering advertisements. If you apply to enough people, you are likely to find the opportunity you seek.

Learn to write a letter of application well. Be sure that you can present yourself honestly and attractively both in interviews and in writing. If you know your abilities, you do not fool yourself about your capacity to do a certain job. See that you actually are well prepared for the job for which you are applying. If the kind of job that you want is one in which it is possible to practice your skill at home, do so. Be *certain* that you really can do the thing that you say you can do. Then put into simple words what your assets are and what your training has been.

Practice at home what you plan to say to the employment manager. Acquire a quiet, assured manner. Learn to describe your abilities without either boasting or apologizing. Be able to meet an employer with confidence. He will do his best to be friendly and helpful. Remember, his company is just as eager to find the right person as you are to find the right job.

Come to an interview dressed conservatively and in good taste. Show that you have confidence in yourself by walking straight and not slouching, by talking straightforwardly, by

213

answering questions thoughtfully. Sometimes you are given an opportunity to ask questions. It is well to know enough about a position to be able to ask some intelligent questions which show that you are interested in the business as a whole, not concerned only about the particular job you want or the salary you will get. Show what you have to *contribute* as well as what you want them to *give* you.

Show that you are willing to listen to the employer's suggestions. For instance, you might be applying for a position selling dresses in a department store, and the employer might suggest that, because of your inexperience, it would be wiser for you to sell at the notions counter first. Accept his advice cordially. Be willing to take whatever tests he suggests and do your best on them. Do not be too concerned if you find that you are nervous. Companies always allow, in test results, for the fact that most prospective employees are ill at ease during a test. Whether you are given a position or not, remember always to thank a prospective employer for talking with you. If you are courteous and do not act as though you were annoyed or desperate because you did not secure the position upon the initial interview, you will probably leave him with a pleasant impression of you. This is a satisfactory interview; it makes the employer decide, "I want to see that girl again."

Keeping Your Job

If you have a position that you like, get some satisfaction out of it instead of thinking of your work as a duty thrust upon you. Think of it as a game of skill in which you can continually improve. Make the job yours by doing it differently—and better—than it has been done before. Do not

214

be discouraged with the job as you find it. Hunt for something new in it daily. It may be possible for you to discover new and more efficient ways of performing routine tasks. Never take the attitude that you know all about a job. See your present position in relation to your broader ambitions.

See your job as a whole, but decide to do one thing at a time and to do it well. If responsibility is given you, meet it, no matter how difficult this may be. Should carrying your new responsibility creditably involve further education or training, don't begrudge giving up some leisure time for study which advances you in your work. Learn to discriminate between what is important and what is trivial in your job. To do this, you must know your work thoroughly. Be a dependable worker. In most jobs, it is poor policy to have spurts of energy and then to be lazy for days. What counts is the steadiness with which you can work without lowering the quality of your work.

Do not make it necessary for your employer to keep a constant check on you to see that you are doing your job. If he has to resort to use of his authority in order to force you to finish your work on time, you have no reason to complain of this unpleasantness. You have, in all probability, gotten only the use of authority, the show of force, that you deserved. On the other hand, do not allow fear of authority to make you bluff or become unable to exercise any initiative.

In holding or advancing in a job, a girl is greatly handicapped if she has formed habits of fear or hostility. Then her relationships with others are generally characterized either by domination or by submission. She may fail at the job, not because she is *incapable* of doing it, but because she *feels* inadequate. Even the prospect of advancement may be frightening. A fearful person may be generally submissive—in fact, a veritable "yes man"—to the "boss," but may prove a petty tyrant to her co-workers or her "inferiors." She may tattle, criticize excessively, or attack people viciously, especially when she feels she's been "kicked around." She may feel this way often, because such people are chronic complainers and quick to take offense even at well-meant criticism.

A person like this can neither respond positively to authority, nor can she exercise authority over others. She cannot *win* authority, for she fears real competition. She prefers to form alliances and pressure groups whose aim is to gain status or salary without having to prove one's worth.

These attitudes are reinforced if this individual is judged, at home, entirely by a material standard: How much money does she earn? How much money can she spend for clothes, for pleasure, or for status for herself and her family in relation to other people in her social group or her neighborhood? The work history of people like this is often marked by numerous job changes, frequent conflicts with employers, co-workers, and subordinates, as well as by a great deal of absence and illness and more than the normal number of accidents.

A good worker has confidence in herself. She enjoys working with others. She is able to give credit where it is due. She has learned how to work with people in authority over her. She evaluates her work realistically; therefore, she is not surprised or frightened if other people criticize it. She sees and acknowledges her limitations, but she recognizes and respects the ability she possesses.

You, as a competent worker, must have faith in your own

ideas. Do not spend your time going around looking for someone else's. On the other hand, do not become over-aggressive or abusive if your ideas do not seem appropriate or are not accepted as a solution to some particular problem. They may be good ideas, but a more experienced person may have recognized that you have overlooked some factors that would present obstacles and make your ideas difficult to apply.

Be willing to talk over the problems in your job with your superiors; they are there to encourage and help you. Do not be embarrassed when you do not know all the answers to questions that are asked you. Take the attitude that you have much to learn. There are many things that you are not expected to know; after all, no two people have had the same experiences. Do not, however, be content not to know. If you find yourself needing additional information, go and get it.

If you can learn these ways of work, you will build up an attitude of trust between yourself and your superiors. Such trust is not created, however, by making yourself into a yes man—a person who agrees only in order to please. Employers who employ only puppets are not likely to help you to progress in your work. Seek a job that strengthens rather than weakens your personality. Most employers like their employees to feel free to express their honest convictions when questioned. None, however, will stand for gossip or betrayed confidences.

You will find that you gain a great deal of security from a job well done. In addition to its bringing you personal satis-faction, work that you enjoy will be your safety valve. Often when personal difficulties or griefs are yours to face, you need distraction from your thoughts, rather than rest. Nothing can provide this distraction more effectively than your work.

Never be afraid to work hard. Plenty of people work very hard and love it. If you have a breakdown from overwork, this is usually a symptom or a result of failure somewhere else in your life. You may have been trying to convince yourself that you could do a job for which you were not fitted, and a breakdown is your escape from it. Or you may have been attracting attention to yourself for so long by telling people how overworked you were that you began to believe your tale yourself. You may need to do a different kind of work, rather than less work.

If It's Not the Right Job

Up to this point the discussion has been primarily from the point of view of the girl who is free to choose a job. Most states extend by law a girl's school preparation until she is sixteen, seventeen, or eighteen years of age, thus postponing her job placement and also preventing her from working at jobs which may be physically harmful to young people. However, some girls have to take the first jobs they can find as soon as they are old enough to work. Other girls may have no chance for further training after high school. Perhaps the families of such girls need money, and the girls must contribute immediately to the family income. Perhaps, because of illness or other family crisis, both their presence at home and their financial support are needed. Because of economic necessity, some girls even have to leave school to go to work. There are even some young people who, with training, are unable to find the right jobs.

How can a girl build a satisfactory life when she has a job for which she is unsuited? Everyone needs the sense of achievement that work gives, the satisfaction to be secured through promotion in a job, the feeling of social responsibility and of having found a place in the world. There are few substitutes for the satisfaction of holding a rewarding job.

However, a girl can make several very positive adjustments when she holds a job in which she is unhappy because her abilities are not utilized. First, she will regard her situation as temporary while she plans to train herself in a specialized skill which will equip her for a different job. She will investigate all the possibilities for training in her community. She may then plan to attend night school classes which offer the vocational skill she wishes to cultivate. Or she may find such classes at the local high school, at a municipal college or business college, at the community center, or at schools which teach trades and industrial arts.

The skill she chooses to learn will not have been thoughtlessly chosen. She will have seriously studied the occupational field—and herself—as suggested in earlier sections of this chapter. She will have chosen a skill which suits her interests, her abilities, and her personality. She will have gained some tryout experience, possibly by working at night or week ends, because she will have reasoned that she does not want to invest time and money learning to do something else which she may not enjoy. Consequently, when she begins her training, she works wholeheartedly, because she knows what she wants.

Another intelligent adjustment for a girl whose job does not challenge her sufficiently is to find, outside her job, an interest in life which becomes so important that it provides

219

the focus for a new organization of life habits. A girl can become so involved in an activity, such as music, dramatics, art, a craft, photography, or athletics, that her constant, all-absorbing effort to gain skill in it results in the development of the same habits of care, concentration, foresight, and ingenuity which successful workers learn. A girl gains from such skill genuine satisfaction in achievement and an experience in self-discipline akin to that which a vocation might give—and which, she may discover, she can apply to the "job" itself.

A girl may even find that she can earn money by means of her interest or hobby. One girl became so skilled in taking pictures of children that her week-end appointments became more lucrative than her regular job. Another girl baked and decorated cakes for special occasions. Another designed and made hats. Another became noted for her ceramic jewelry.

Physical exercise, also, is helpful to a girl. By this means, she can get rid of the tension which builds up as a feeling of frustration grows. If a girl takes up active sports, such as basketball, swimming, or tennis, she will not be so likely to "blow up" or to remain depressed.

Understanding of herself—knowing why she feels and acts as she does—will assist a wise girl during a difficult period when, because her family needs her or her economic help, she must accept a job "not good enough" for her. Is she facing the situation, or is she responding by rebelling against the family, by dominating younger brothers and sisters, or by blaming her parents for her plight? Some girls, unable to "take it," have walked out on their families, run away from home, or hitchhiked across the country. Others have attempted to escape by becoming physically or mentally ill.

Active sports release tension and give you opportunities to experience many personal satisfactions.

Still other girls have made martyrs out of themselves by refusing to see their former friends; they felt that they were no longer "good enough" to associate with them. Such depreciation of themselves has caused some girls to refuse dates, to take out their disappointment on girl friends, to wear mannish clothes, or to pose as "intellectuals."

Naturally, a girl in this situation *will* suffer keenly if she is unable to remain part of "the gang." Many a girl will be tempted to yield to apathy, defeatism, disillusionment, lack of interest in active sports, reluctance to meet people, failure even to keep up former friendships. Fortunately, however, there is in human beings a powerful instinct to gain relief from frustration and uncertainty by participating in whatever activities are still open to them.

Every girl *can* develop an intelligent plan of action. She can master new skills which will assure her a future different from her present. She can develop interests and recreational activities which will build up her self-respect. She can take advantage of every opportunity to associate with boys and girls socially—at work, at night school, at church, at community clubs or centers, and in friends' homes—confident that her friends enjoy being with her and doing things with her because she is making herself, continually, into a more interesting person. Such a girl has no time to feel sorry for herself!

Getting Ahead in the Job

Most of you are eager to succeed in the world; you want to win friends and get along well in your business and social relationships. You feel that, to stand high in the esteem of your family, friends, and community, you must work toward a good job or toward promotion in your present job. In your struggle for a satisfying life and a successful career, you work in two areas: with yourself and with your environment. Perhaps you can do little to change your environment, but you *can* improve yourself. You can learn increasingly to adjust your personality to the demands of the people with whom you work and to the requirements of the world in which you live and work.

For better or for worse, you shape your job. Almost everyone wants to be "tops" in her job, or at least wants to move ahead. Yet the quality of a job can be no better than the quality of the person holding it. The amount of satisfaction your job will give you is largely up to you. No one can be directed into a job *guaranteeing* a happy, effective life. You can, however, grow on your job. You can develop into a person with the maturity and flexibility to solve new problems as they are presented.

You can envision your future as one in which you *have learned to function in the vocational world.* You can strive to adapt to a world of work, not simply to a mass of skills! You can understand this *broader* role as against the round-peg-in-round-hole concept of adapting to *a* job.

Plan your future. Set up a goal, and never lose sight of it! Your goal must be realistic and practical in terms of what you, as a total person, may become. Then you can think ahead intelligently: What work habits, personality characteristics, skills, techniques, and knowledge must you have in order to advance toward your goal? How can you arrange your present work in order to learn more about the job you want in the future?

Generally, young people change jobs several times before they feel that they have *the* job. However, some young people are too hasty in considering a current job a "blind alley." The "blind alley" may be in your mind! Explore your job thoroughly; give it as much range and depth as your training will permit. You may find that the job changes as you change. No one adapts to a situation intelligently without the situation, in some way, adapting to the person.

If you are a perceptive individual, you will soon discover that personality traits and characteristics outweigh all other considerations in determining the degree to which people succeed or fail in their chosen work. Personality, obviously, cannot take the place of intelligence or training, but it certainly influences how far the person of adequate intelligence and training will rise. The fact that personality characteristics are basic—in initial employment, in promotion, advancement, or discharge—can be a challenge. The wise person will accept this challenge. She will honestly face herself, and then she will discipline herself to change those traits and habits which are undesirable. You know now that personality *can* be improved.

What are some of the personal characteristics which employers consider essential in an effective employee? Most frequently mentioned are good work habits. *Dependability* includes being on time, doing a full day's work, and offering to give extra time or help when necessary. *Efficiency* means doing assigned work quickly and correctly. It means not dawdling, not using company time for personal letters or grooming, not using the company telephone for personal calls. *Initiative* means intelligently listening to directions, then working on one's own, making one's own minor decisions, and persevering in a job until one has finished it creditably. *Reliability* means carrying through on one's promises honestly and without bluffing. It means admitting mistakes and seeking help as necessary. *Congeniality* includes ability to get along smoothly with co-workers, with supervisors, with the public, and with the people in subordinate positions. It implies ability to take criticism well and to give it helpfully. It implies willingness to do one's share of the work, to be cooperative when suggestions are made, and to be interested in other people and their work. It involves courtesy, tact, neatness, and good health habits.

The basic issue in planning toward one's future is the relationship between personality and technique. Major attention should be given to what you are as a person. The techniques you acquire should be used as means of strengthening your personality. They should be methods which enable you to function more humanly and more warmly (therefore more effectively) because you comprehend clearly the relationship of your work and that of your colleagues. Only when you become *involved,* actually absorbed in the importance of what you are doing, can you feel satisfaction, in your work. As you *gain* this satisfaction, you *give* satisfaction to your employer.

Some girls see their futures in terms of jobs that will do something for them. This value is upside down. The mature girl sees her future in terms of what she can contribute to a job to make it better, to make it go where she believes with all her being it ought to go. The enthusiasm, initiative, courage, and judgment you bring to a job open to you opportunity for progress in your chosen field. If you have the attitude "I want to feel that what I'm doing matters" or "I want to contribute something of myself and my education," you will not just fill some niche every morning and leave it each night as you found it. You will help build and shape your job. As you grow in judgment and resolution, your job will grow. You will have demonstrated your ability to excel and progress with it.

You may not know what the future of your job will be or whether it will have a future; some 6,000 new occupations were born in the last fifteen years. Moreover, 3 out of 5 jobs created since 1940 are filled by women, many of them housewives past forty years of age. Part-time jobs have increased 40 per cent since 1957. Women now make up one-third of the work force. Girls have choices for the use of their abilities which range from serving others locally, nationally, and internationally to assisting in building rockets to the moon.

CHAPTER NINE

Life Is More Than a Job

WHAT WILL YOU BE DOING after high school? Some of you will at once have to answer the question, "How shall I make a living?" You will, of course, want a job which is interesting and profitable and which affords you some success and recognition as a contributing member of your community.

Of course, you will seek a job which is right in terms of your abilities and the demands of the job. However, not many jobs in modern society will offer you sufficient challenge to fulfill all your expectations of life. Must you, then, resign yourself to boredom?

Those of you who are truly growing up will find that life is more than a job. You will seek to answer not only the question, "How can I make a living?" but also the more basic one, "How can I go on building my life?" Your answer to the last question will depend as much upon your *use* of your ability and of what you have learned as it will upon the amount of ability you have or the amount you have learned. The end of your formal schooling need not be the end of learning. It can be the beginning of a new kind of learning.

How can you build your life? Your daily experience is your raw material. Use it to goad yourself to reach out—to develop your mind, your body, your interests, your circle of friends, and your values. Your experience has many aspects. Let us examine three: (1) Time is your first raw material, probably your most precious one. Twenty-four hours every day are yours to fill or to leave empty of value. (2) Your potentialities are your second raw material. Will you fulfill them? From an unending, rich diversity of activities—physical and mental, available to anyone—will you make the effort to learn how to do well things that are worth doing? (3) Your third raw material is the challenge facing you daily. Because you live constantly with other people, learn skill in working with people. Your generation must pioneer in this area, for the frontiers of the human mind and heart are unexplored. If you can widen and deepen your feeling of kinship with others and learn to see underneath the surface and identify new wellsprings of energy, technique, and faith, then individuals of divergent backgrounds will be able to talk, think, plan, and work together.

Is it possible to challenge teen-agers to build lives which will be of significance to themselves and to others? Some people point to complications. It has been said that today's teen-agers have greater mobility than any previous generation—but do they know where they want to go or how they want to spend their time? They are affluent beyond the imaginings of Croesus, but do they know where their wealth really comes from, how long it will last, or what to do with it?

227

They are bombarded continually with advertising and information, yet are they sure how much of what they are told can be believed? Common denominators seem to get lower and more common. How can they learn to discriminate among values? How can they cut through the junk of our culture and learn to winnow out the superficial from the real? How can they look behind the clutter of words for their true meaning and find out how they are sometimes being manipulated?

What will you answer? You can take a stand: I will make the most of my experiences; I will learn to comprehend my environment; in each twenty-four hours, I will look for opportunities to build something new and important into my life.

As the poet Gregory Corso says, "They got machines now to do the work. People got to start thinking. That's what's going to save us." Will you be among those who start thinking?

Your Use of Time

Each of you has struggled, more or less conscientiously, to prepare yourself for what you cannot foresee—the actual job by which you will earn your living. Any day, a new mechanical device may be invented to do the work which now requires your careful training. Yet you keep on using your time and intelligence to ready yourself for the job— and rightly so. But do you use as much intelligence and time to prepare yourself for something you *can* foresee—the fact that you will have much free time after working hours?

Not much has been said to you in school about this matter. Adults, in general, did not realize how quickly this situation would grow into a major problem in our culture. The use of free time may not now seem a problem to you, accustomed as you are to crowded high school days. However, your earning-a-living job may absorb only thirty hours or less a week! In fact, one mathematician predicts that, twenty-five years from now, 2 per cent of our population will produce all the goods and food that the other 98 per cent can consume!

The problem of choosing what you will do with leisure time is, therefore, very real. Now, leisure is not only available to everyone; it will be forced upon everyone. How will *you* prepare to use it? Your mental health and your happiness depend upon your answer to this question.

The Age of Leisure is bound to produce a marvelous world of comforts and luxuries. We possess the tools to create whatever kind of world we want. Many people, up to now, have spent their time, money, and energy in accumulating material things only. Some "newly rich" people acquire things merely as status symbols, not for their intrinsic value. They want to prove to their neighbors that they "worked for it" or that they are successful, perhaps "better than" their neighbors! Some such people have concentrated all their time on work; they are suspicious of leisure. They believe implicitly Carlyle's dictate that "work is alone noble." Americans spring from a long line of compulsive go-getters! Some of us have forgotten the Biblical injunction: there is also a time to laugh and a time to dance.

Other people, however, believe in excellence rather than in status; they work more for their own satisfaction and for the esteem of their peers rather than for material reward. Consider the numbers of young people volunteering for the Peace Corps, the Agency for International Development, or for

229

comparable opportunities to help people in our country and throughout the world. Not only are these individuals exempt from the pressure to use their energies to "get ahead," they also find pleasure and self-renewal in both their work and their leisure time. What could be more important to happiness? In fact, writes John Gardner, "Continuous renewal is the price of survival."

What does he mean by this? We all need to set aside some time to enrich our lives and spirits, time to be alone; we need to work at something we enjoy, to think, to read, to become acquainted with ourselves. You are living in a fast-paced world. Many conflicting demands are made on everyone; many appeals are made to each of you to invest your interest and effort in this or that project. You need sufficient time with yourself to know yourself and to cultivate that self. How can you make wise decisions about how you will use your life unless you know what you want out of life? How can you confidently know what you have to offer unless you have cultivated an inner self you can respect? True, some people are afraid to be alone—perhaps because they face only emptiness when they face themselves. Do you discover an interesting, enjoyable companion when you face yourself?

All your life, you will be choosing between flabby, easy, and effortless use of free time and the use of these free hours to some advantage. You *can* choose to do nothing with your free time; you can just "set," or you can use time for trivialities which lead to boredom and the sure death of your creative possibilities. In this case, all you will develop is skill in the art of killing time. On the other hand, you can develop a balance between the demands of your daytime job and those of your leisure interests. Start to hunt for commitments that

230

will bring personal rewards and permanent satisfactions, not just for something to fill time.

When you shift your sights, you will not only discover a variety of ways in which you can make yourself a more creative and interesting person, but you will also find all around you in your community mountains of unfinished business. For example, how much time and energy will it take to beautify our cities? abolish our slums? develop recreation areas? give everyone the opportunity to learn all he wants to learn?

Remember, the amount of time given you each day is rationed. You may increase your cash income, but by no amount of effort or luck can you increase your amount of time. All of your life you will have only twenty-four hours a day. An increasing number of these hours will be free time. At the end of a day, will you be forced to admit that you squandered those free hours somewhere, somehow in aimless and casual pastimes?

Your Use of Money

Teen-agers handle a great deal of money. Many are given allowances; a growing number earn money in part-time jobs. Girls spend money mostly on clothing, cosmetics, jewelry, records, and amusements. No wonder that, when you consider what you will do with your free time, you think about money. You may even decide that you cannot do much with your time unless you have money.

Obviously, the spending of money is dynamite. To spend or not to spend is not the only question. You need to understand the techniques of advertising so that you will not be misled by the whipped-up appeals to prejudice, false standards, poor taste, or pride in inverted values which sometimes

231

are involved in the psychology of buying and selling. You need to learn, by trial and error, that some things are not worth the money invested in them. Intelligent spending, in other words, assumes that you are grown-up enough to know that you do not need to buy and buy in order to prove to yourself and others that you can spend whatever you want and accumulate whatever you wish from the wealth of things you are urged to acquire.

There is plenty of pressure on you to squander time—and money—on pastimes provided ready-made by people in the business of providing you entertainment and recreation. Leisure interests of young people have become increasingly commercialized. In some places, you pay even to bowl, ski, skate, or canoe. You spend much of your free time in movies or at passive, ready-made amusements which you buy at a price.

In fact, manufacturers and advertisers influence almost every phase of your life. They make their livings urging you to spend more and more of your time and money buying and using material objects—their products, of course. Your clothes, your hair-do, your speech, the songs you sing, the records you listen to, and the dances you learn are those advertised in magazines, featured in movies, publicized on television. By frequent style changes, manufacturers also make sure that your purchases are discarded long before their usefulness is exhausted. You can't be seen in last year's models!

This situation is not due to the selfishness of one group of people desiring to exploit another. The fact is that money has become the sole medium of exchange in our society, and for some it has become an end rather than a means. If you realize this, you will not be hampered by money, nor will you feel helplessly dependent on it. Money alone cannot secure you desirable objects or living conditions. Some people spend so much time, energy, and intelligence in superfluous buying and owning of possessions or in eagerly seeking excitement and amusement that they lose sight of this fact: Your time, energy, and intelligence are yours to use as you please; you do not have to be influenced by the pressures of those who offer you their wares. You know that the cash in your pocket is not your only tool for the creation of a satisfying life!

What is your alternative? It is to learn early that the satisfaction of your deepest desires—for companionship, emotional poise, new experiences, recognition of your skills and abilities—seldom depends on the spending of money. You rob yourself if you assume that nothing is worth doing unless it involves a money reward or that precious values can be had only for cash. In fact, you are likely to get more satisfaction out of doing things or making things than out of purchasing them. Look for activities that can give you tangible things you want and, in addition, enjoyment of the companionship of friends with similar interests. You have health and few restrictions on your free time. If you have imagination also, you can become an actress or magician, a cook, a guitar player, creator and manager of a puppet theater, a swimmer, a gardener, a skier, a skater, a skin diver. You can design and make your own dresses, hats and accessories. You can experiment in interior decorating as you learn to beautify your own room. You and your friends can give musical and dramatic performances. You can learn photography and become expert in certain areas, such as taking pictures of children, or animals, or flowers. You can bicycle and picnic in the parks and surrounding country. You can hike or study birds in nearby hills and woods, or camp beside the lakes. You can fish, canoe, row in the streams, climb or ski in the mountains.

Day camping and hosteling have opened up tremendous possibilities for the use of the natural surroundings near you. Each season of the year has its offerings for both individual and group leisure-time activities.

Suppose your community affords no opportunity that appeals to you. Then you and your friends will have to make the opportunities. Young people can unite their energies in projects for community betterment. Skating rinks for both summer and winter can be developed. Unused lots can be made into sports areas. Certain designated park areas can be turned into space for various athletics. Teen-age centers can be opened with the help of adult sponsorship. Space and leadership can be found for day camps. Some of these activities, it is true, will call for money, but in most cases the chief ingredients for their success are the imagination, industry, and cooperation of the young people who initiate and maintain them. Through do-it-yourself projects, boys and girls in many communities have demonstrated the fact that, if you are willing to work hard for something, you can usually get what you want. The achievement of projects for community betterment will give you the deepest satisfaction. The actual doing of them will be fun and will enable you honestly to lay a higher value upon your own abilities. You will discard, once and for all, the false idea that you can use your leisure time enjoyably and profitably only when you are spending money to buy possessions or amusement.

Your Use of Your Potentialities

As you join in activities like these, you develop interests and learn to use your potentialities. Activity which challenges you, interests which result in tangible accomplishments and the development of new skills—all of these will be your reward for putting thought and effort into the way in which you use your leisure time. What a paycheck will buy in material possessions will not give you these satisfactions. Nor will you gain them by passively killing time in amusements provided by others. You do not need relaxation at the end of your work day. You need activity. In fact, everyone wants to be active, to feel useful, to create or achieve something peculiarly her own. Life is not neatly divided between work and "mere recreation." If leisure is to serve its function of re-creation, it must be more than aimless play.

How do you develop interests? Sometimes from intellectual curiosity about people and things, sometimes from gregariousness—a desire to be with people and do what they are doing! Usually, you begin with the questions "What? How? Where? Why?" Then you do something about finding answers to these questions. You do not only make feeble gestures with your mind; you develop intellectual curiosity. You actively seek to know.

As a strong interest in something develops, new aspects unfold and new ideas multiply and unexpected tie-ups with other interests are revealed. For example, the scientist George Washington Carver asked, "What's in a peanut?" He used his mind and laboratory skill to find out. He discovered thirty products; yet, he assured his students, the humble peanut still held many secrets, any one of which might start a train of investigation in the chemical field to which it was related. Clearly, if you do try to find answers to your questions, you will develop your potentialities and master a variety of skills. Thus your interests can grow into absorbing hobbies, genuine accomplishments, or even into your life work.

Skills and interests are not acquired by mere random fun—important though fun is. You work hard at something which interests you. Through persistent effort, you acquire skill at a task. Moreover, you will drive on to perfect your skill in a chosen field or fields just for the satisfaction you gain in accomplishment. Satisfaction in achievement is a fundamental source of your happiness and self-confidence. As you learn to do something well, you nourish your personality; you gain self-respect as you receive from others recognition of your ability.

If you have a sincere desire to use your potentialities, you will find or make opportunities to do so. Teen-agers all over the country have organized community groups where they study and develop skills in whatever interests them—writing short stories, designing airplanes, organizing little theaters or dance bands, collecting stamps, refinishing furniture. The list of activities is long and varied. One group pooled their money to equip an art workshop with facilities for leatherwork, weaving, wood carving, sculpture, painting and jewelry making, using silver, copper, enamel, and ceramics.

You may plan in your free time to gain skill in other areas. Perhaps you are interested in learning to read and speak a foreign language well because, some day, you will be traveling, living, or working abroad. You may want to take up chemistry because you became interested in nutrition. Where can you learn these things? Public night schools and community colleges are available to thousands of young people. Universities and colleges, technical schools, community agencies, religious organizations, chambers of commerce, labor unions, and farmer and professional people's organizations stand ready and willing to provide leadership to help you. Many will assist you in sponsoring a series of films or discussions or forums on topics of interest to you. The League of

Women Voters, for example, is intensely interested in helping women become informed on public questions. Some state universities include centers for continued study. Their offerings range from two- or three-day seminars on campus to courses that may take several weeks or months to complete, and from correspondence courses to traveling libraries and centers for distribution of educational films. Your local library will help you generously as you seek to develop new interests and skills. If you have no local library, call on your state library. You will be furnished with reference information, books, and films for nothing but the cost of postage.

The opportunity to learn is open to you from birth to death. The cost in money is negligible. Imagination, industry, interest, and the ability to recognize and use an opportunity are the chief requisites. The scope and range for development of your potentialities and skills is enormous. You need only to make the effort to fit the opportunities to your interests and aspirations, using flexibility and accuracy in your planning. If you do, you will find that you like mental workouts, that you enjoy learning new skills or finding answers to problems which have stumped you, that you want what is going on in this vastly exciting world to be intelligible to you, that you enjoy meeting interesting people, that it is fun to try out your ideas on people—in short, that life without something interesting to do and think and learn is dull.

Your Skill in Working with People

In earlier chapters it was emphasized that, as human beings, we all share certain basic needs and that our behavior is governed by basic laws. Suppose you apply these laws to your behavior: starting with the assumption that there must be some reason for your behavior, you find, if you are honest with yourself, that you can discover why you feel and act as you do.

Little by little, you learn to appraise both your strengths and your weaknesses. Frequently, you find that your weaknesses are not due to actual defects of character, but to poor techniques. For example, suppose you have a hot temper and easily let bitter words fly. This is not an inheritance that will dog you always but a bad habit, a lack of self-control, a poor technique which you can learn to change. The discovery that you can manage your own nature results in your beginning to count on yourself.

Although you do not close your eyes to your faults, you cease to fear them, be ashamed of them, or feel frustrated because you cannot conquer them all and achieve perfection. You neither praise nor blame yourself so often; you become less elated over some success, less depressed by some failure. Then, because you can believe in yourself, you are able to believe in other people. As you understand *your* personality needs, you deepen your sensitivity to the needs of others.

When you face your *own* limitations and can be fair to yourself, then you can be fair to other people. If you are tolerant of your own failures and respect yourself in spite of them, you will not yield to cynicism or stoop to blaming others when you fail. In other words, as you understand and accept yourself with your limitations, you are freed of yourself. You no longer need be self-centered—occupied solely with yourself and your own problems. Thus, as you learn to respect yourself, you become able to respect other people.

More important, you actively try to understand others. You don't dismiss as "stupid and narrow-minded" someone who disagrees with you. You realize that, if you are actually more nearly right, the difference lies in the fact that you have learned a technique for handling prejudice and fear; you have learned to think straight. When you examined your own behavior, you found that the roots of ignorance, prejudice, and frustration lay in anger and fear. You reasoned that growing up meant learning to guide your emotions so that fears and anger yielded to thinking. Thinking is not necessarily orderly or even honest; your thought processes do not automatically go in a straight line. But you can train yourself to think straight: Look for facts about ideas and things you had thoughtlessly feared; learn to know people against whom you have previously been blindly prejudiced. As you do so, you find yourself enjoying people whom you formerly considered "different." You realize that you are asking questions about ideas which formerly frightened you, that you are looking for answers which make more sense to you than the fears and prejudices you had unquestioningly nursed all these years.

As you become aware of reasons behind *your* ignorance, prejudices, and fears, you begin to understand how and why other people arrive at *their* opinions. Now, when you become impatient with other people's stubbornness and narrowness, you do not feel superior to them; you remind yourself how long it took you to discover similar attitudes in yourself and how you are still struggling to overcome them. You share your techniques and try, by example, to help others grow in understanding.

All the while that you are trying to learn more about yourself and others, you must day by day *use* what you now know. Life must be lived with whatever wisdom you can muster. It does not stop to give you time to learn "all the answers";

you must use what knowledge you have and cope as best you can today, even as you are in the act of acquiring more knowledge in order to cope better tomorrow.

Suppose you find yourself in a difficult home, neighborhood, or school situation. Can you improve what you find—even as you accept what you cannot presently change? Can you help the situation to progress from where it is to something better while, at the same time, learning as much as possible from today's problems?

In other words, constructive day-by-day living means *applying* to daily living what you know of human nature even as you are *adding* to your knowledge of it. In our culture this skill is shown in your growing ability to live, learn, and work *democratically* with others. How do you stack up in these areas? Do you treat others with courtesy and consideration? Do you form and express opinions and help others to do so? Do you use your talents for the common good? Do you both exercise good leadership and follow it? Do you encourage it in others? Do you know how to reject poor leadership, how to respect individual personality, and how to mobilize the best in each environment toward the greatest good?

Opportunity to exercise this skill is furnished you every hour of your life. Democracy is not merely a form of government; it is a *way of life* which works—in your family, your school and your neighborhood—only if people are willing to learn how to make it work. It is not a theory but a method, one that can be learned only by hard work, patience, and intelligence. It involves willingness to accept responsibility for the freedom you demand—and willingness to give others the same freedom. Should you demand freedom to say what you like, remember that others also have the right to demand freedom to say what *they* like, even in criticism of you. Your

240

free speech involves, then, your learning to be careful about *what* you say.

Your student council should be an excellent base for learning skill in working with people. To the degree that your council is effective, it gives you opportunities for forming and expressing opinions, for exchanging opinions with others who have different points of view, for learning to judge your opinions in the light of theirs, for learning to disagree and to be disagreed with without becoming disagreeable. It gives you opportunity to follow your leaders intelligently, to exercise leadership, to choose good and reject poor leadership. It teaches you how to vote and how to hold office. It gives you experience in school and community service of many kinds. It provides opportunities for you to become acquainted with, and to work with, boys and girls with many types of ability and background. It provides you practice in helping them to use their individual talents for the common good, practice in treating them with respect and consideration. You learn to take part in frank and full discussion of problems facing the school community. You learn to accept a decision made by the majority even when you do not agree with it. You may not feel that the decision made or the action taken is necessarily the best or the only solution to the problem, but you support the action because you understand it. You have learned that out of broad, general discussion grows a unity that makes for cooperation, that assures action, and that assumes loyalty to the action. You come to realize that a kind of unity is possible even in the midst of diversity and that, even though the members of a group may not agree in all details, they can plan an intelligent attack on a problem and learn the habit of approaching problems with an honest desire to "see all sides."

241

You can find many opportunities in your home, school, and neighborhood to practice skill in working with people. Try yourself out in family discussions, in homeroom and club meetings in school, in the community or teen-age center, in church committees, in forums or junior town meetings. Participate wherever you can in the organization and functioning of groups; these are deliberate actions in our democracy—part and parcel of our characteristically democratic process of making up our minds.

If you deliberately seek a wide variety of experiences with people, you will learn to work and play with boys, girls, and adults of different religions, races, nationalities, political affiliations, and social and economic backgrounds. You will learn to know boys and girls in public and private schools. You will learn to work with adults in a shared responsibility for the welfare of a home, school, and community. You may be surprised to discover how much all these people are alike, how insignificant are the superficial differences between them that you saw—and perhaps feared—at first.

As you gain skill in working with people, take time to appraise what you are doing in each group in which you participate. Are you adding to your skill? For example, when you move to a new school or community and join a club, certain ideas and interests may be new to you. Do you learn something about these ideas and how to make yourself competent in some field of interest pertaining to them? Or do you voice opinions formed from hearsay, prejudice, hit-or-miss reading or halfhearted attention to what has been said in a movie or on a television program? Voicing opinions publicly carries responsibility for making accurate statement of facts. If you find it difficult to form unbiased opinions, teach yourself to gather facts. Read, and listen to and question people who hold views contrary to your own and then form your opinions. As a participant in a group, you are under obligation to learn the skill of listening to and contributing intelligently to frank and full discussion of all that interests and concerns members of the group. How skillful are you? Do you find it difficult to disagree in a discussion without becoming disagreeable? Do you confuse facts with your personal opinions or arguments with personal remarks? Do you grow angry if someone hints that your opinions aren't worth much? If you do, avail yourself of the practice that group discussion offers in developing self-control and open-mindedness. These skills are basic in working effectively with people.

During a group discussion, you may get a new angle on a subject, or you may confirm your own opinion. Whether a discussion alters or confirms your personal opinion matters less than your understanding of the significance of discussion. After a genuine "meeting of minds," everyone recognizes the desire of everyone else to find the truth, not just to silence someone or to prove herself smarter than someone else.

Somehow you feel akin to people with whom you have talked something out; you may not agree with them, but you understand them. You have learned that you can respect, like, and appreciate people who do not look, act, and think as you do. When you first feel this way, you will have taken an important step toward mastering the skill of working with people. Simultaneously, you are beginning to learn the responsibilities and the benefits of citizenship in a land made up of many people with a wide diversity of needs, aspirations, and points of view.

CHAPTER TEN

The Give-and-Take
of Living

IF GROWING UP is the process by which you progress from egocentricity to socialization, then *maturity* describes your ability progressively to take your place in the world. How mature you are depends on how successfully you have made some of the important adjustments in life. It is not always easy to make these adjustments. People who are blocked in making adjustments, even those people who remain at childish levels because they have found the grown-up way too difficult, deserve sympathy. But you will not want to accept the easy way. You will want to keep your personality —and your "self"—growing as you learn from your mistakes and from those of others.

Finding Yourself

If you want to be a mature, happy, well-adjusted individual, you must find a place for yourself in life. Most basic of all, you must find security; you must have a self that you can depend on. You must be a person who is self-confident, who expects to be successful, and who really is successful fairly often. How are you to develop such a self? Some of the ways

244

have been explained in this book. Summarized briefly these ways are as follows: Know your abilities, and be eager to try them out. Confront the new and different with attitudes of eagerness and optimism, not of fear and resentment. See the untried as material for your enlarging experience. Understand your limitations and handicaps; see them as a challenge. Use your energies—set your will—to improve yourself. Substitute things that you can do for those that you cannot, thus compensating in a constructive manner for what you cannot alter. Meet your failures and your difficulties with courage and confidence. Face, rather than escape or deplore, the problems of life. Understand your problems, but do not let them discourage you.

Recognize in yourself evidences of second-rate behavior such as that which was described in Chapter 3. Deal with such behavior effectively; have the power of guidance over your fears, anxieties, angers, irritations, resentments, or loves—the power to refrain from selfish reactions and from behavior that may injure others. And remember that it always helps, in dealing with your behavior reactions, to be able to laugh at yourself. Cultivate the ability to concentrate on your present problem. Do not worry; ignore the past and the future, except as they are definitely related to the present.

Keep physically fit. Know and practice the rules of health. Be able also to adjust your daily routine, your way of life, to the amount of strain which you can stand. Do not expect to do more than you are physically able to do. Your failure to observe the rules of physical health may mean financial burdens to others; it will result in inefficiency and unhappiness for yourself, since you lose your self-confidence when you no longer feel that you are able to do things well.

245

Your life purpose. You first begin to look for a guide to your own life when you find that your thoughts are really your personal possessions. You make this discovery when, as you grow older, you frequently find yourself thinking differently from your parents or from other people who have taught you. You may discover that a number of people whom you admire differ from you in their ideas about race, nationality, religion, science, politics, conduct, or education. In fact, your own ideas may seem much more sensible and humane to you than the ideas held by adults who taught you earlier.

Girls meet this problem in various ways. Some girls accept without question the ideas that they have learned at home, at church, or at school. These girls believe that the people in authority over them are always right. Other girls may throw over such ideas only to find themselves baffled by their own independent thinking. They may seek a substitute source of authority in the "gang" or in some other person or institution. Such girls cannot stand uncertainty or growing pains but must have definite answers.

There are also girls who openly disagree with everyone. They may disagree just to show that they have minds of their own or because they have fun in rebelling. The danger in such behavior is that they may keep on merely disagreeing and rebelling all their lives, never coming to any conclusions or gaining any convictions.

Most girls, however, are really groping for some method of deciding what they will live by. Many of you are like the girl who said, "What's life for? You can't grow up without wondering, especially in these days when scientists tell us that if another war comes, at least one out of every three people will be killed by atomic blasts. It scares you. Gosh, if life is that cheap, what's life for, anyway?"

Each of you has to answer that question for herself. And you may be sure that adults understand the fear and the bitterness this girl expressed! Adults are afraid of the future, too. Vera Brittain, writing as long ago as the end of the First World War, expressed this fear when she wrote: "Only gradually did I realize that the war had condemned me to live to the end of my days in a world without confidence or security—in a world in which love would seem perpetually threatened by death, and happiness appear a house without duration, built upon shifting sands of chaos." Modern novels paint discouraging pictures of the futility of life. They mirror the confusion and despair of many adults.

Girls of your age have never experienced a Christmas in which all the whole world was really completely at peace. Your world is threatened by the terrible menace of the hydrogen bomb; international problems enter squarely into your personal life. No wonder people are afraid!

For the first time in the history of the world, the fate of each of us is inextricably and directly bound up with everyone else's. We cannot escape our responsibility for other people. Therefore, over and above the babble about present-day purposeless living, individuals, groups, and whole nations are banding together looking for answers to the question, "What is life for?"

A sense of direction. Linda, one of the girls mentioned in the beginning of this book—recognized the importance of this question when she said, "I guess my trouble is that I don't really know what I want. I can't decide what's best to do about school, about Jack—and Mother. I guess you must have a belief or you don't know where you're going. I used to think that what you believed was something you decided on when you grew up. Now I think you can't go on without knowing—besides, we don't have time to grow up! Look at me. By the way some parents and some schools treat us, you'd think we were babies—but here I am at seventeen trying to decide about the draft and marriage and Mother's future—or maybe I'm just afraid for my own future."

Patti, the other girl in Chapter 1, said: "I don't know why I behave like this. I guess part of it is that school seems kind of futile. Nobody seems to take anything very seriously. Honestly, I think most of the kids don't care about anything—except maybe wheels! Getting wheels, having fun, and 'horsing around'! I 'horse around' a lot too. Maybe I do it to keep from thinking. I can't talk to anyone at home now—but I'm scared. My brother's friends used to argue whether they'd join the reserves or wait for the draft. Then one fellow's brother came home, wounded, from Vietnam. He told us plenty! Americans don't realize what war is these days—and you can't tell some of 'em either. I guess I don't see any future. What's the good of working for or wanting anything?"

Many teen-agers have tough problems to face as they ask themselves what their life is for and what they want out of life. Patti, feeling so alone this year, has had no goal, save to live from day to day. Linda, a child of divorced parents, is attempting to be a contributing member of one family group while, at the same time, she wonders whether she "ought" to take responsibility for her mother.

What Linda, Patti, and *you* are really seeking is a pattern for living. Today, for you, is not good enough. You feel that tomorrow *must* be better, that you are living beneath your capacities, that you are not as effective, not as happy as you can be. If one could only say to you, "It's so simple—just do this and this." However, you know now that no one can give you *the* answer in a nutshell or neatly wrapped in silver paper dripping with tinsel. You can only be helped to develop some sense of direction as you seek your *own* answers.

Linda is reacting honestly as a normal, healthy individual when she admits sadly that she doesn't really want to live with her mother, because she doesn't understand her mother and her mother doesn't understand Linda. Yet Linda feels guilty because she isn't helping her mother and wonders whether, if she lived with her mother, she *could* help more. Linda needs to realize that one cannot live someone else's life, nor can one pick up someone else's pieces for her and mend her broken life. Sacrificing one's life to someone else is not a happy solution for either person. No one can *make* someone else become happier and better adjusted. No one can be *forced* to learn from her mistakes. No one can *be* changed. A person must want to change herself, and if her difficulties are severe she may need professional help, as Linda's mother does, if she is to change.

To help her mother, Linda can only be kind to her, visit her when possible, and try to keep their time together relaxed and pleasant. To help herself, Linda can refrain from judging harshly either her mother or her father, whom she may unconsciously blame for some of her mother's mental illness. But, most important, Linda can learn to face her own problems effectively, so that life will not defeat her.

249

Mental illness is not inherited; it is not something to be ashamed of or to fear. However, one can learn from someone else's unhappiness.

Patti's life is not easy either. She feels rejected by her parents. Being certain of parent's love is basic in developing self-respect. Yet many parents cannot love every boy or girl equally. Parents are people, too, and sometimes they are drawn to one child more than to another; they respond more warmly to one child's looks, temperament, or type of ability.

Sometimes parents' feelings about a child are confused; they only *seem* to prefer one child to another. They may secretly be amused by the "antics" of the noisy, witty, mischievous child, but because of fear of what the neighbors may say they may compare the child, to her own discredit, with the quiet, good child. Or they may admire the child who "always has his fists up" even while they rebuke her and tell her to "look at your brother" who "never fights—why, he won't even take his own part!" Again parents may, at various stages in a child's growth, be more or less interested in her. Some parents who love to dress and care for a baby are horrified by the noise, sloppiness, and dirt dragged into the house by a ten-year-old. Some others who are flattered by a small child's request for help in learning to play ball or ride a bicycle are flabbergasted by a teen-ager's "wild ideas" and flaunting of parental authority.

It is important for everyone to learn that no parent can love every child in the same way. Nevertheless, everyone needs to feel that she *is* loved by, and is important to, her parents. If she cannot have this security, she does not feel that *she* is important. Her behavior will show that she is a troubled, unhappy person. She will resort to the kind of

250

behavior which says distinctly, if its language is understood, "If I can't have approval, I'll settle for attention."

Patti feels twice deserted right now—by her parents and by her brother. When one feels left out at home, it is difficult to reach out toward other people. This year Patti needs her friends more than ever. The film *The Quiet One* shows so well how a boy felt who was truly unwanted and unloved by his parents. He turned to truancy, stealing, and lying. Yet he desperately wanted love, as we all do. "When the human soul is uprooted, it flees from uncertainty to uncertainty, mistrustful of itself, until it is fully accepted by another's understanding." When the boy finally found a counselor and teacher into whose trust he could safely place his need and his love, he began to grow—to move forward *into* life, not backward. Each of us must have someone who loves and trusts us if we are to learn to love and trust others —or ourselves.

If you cannot find this relationship inside your family, you must seek it outside—without bitterness and without feeling that because *your* family was unsatisfactory, family living is unimportant. You need to become mature enough to look at your family, understand why the tensions and unhappiness existed, and resolve to learn from your parents' immaturities and mistakes while you accept your parents for what they are.

When you find a relationship which helps you to grow up and believe in yourself, it will be so important to you that you must struggle with yourself to avoid trying to hold on possessively to the person who makes your growth possible. *Self*-respect is your real goal—and this no one can give you, although other people can *help* you toward it. In the last

251

analysis, regardless of what our parents and friends do *to* us and *for* us, each of us must "walk on" alone with whatever we've built up inside ourselves as our only guide!

It is not easy to find your own answers. No one correct answer will come to you in a trumpet blast from heaven some sunny afternoon between two sets of tennis. Each one of you will have to find your own answers, answers you are willing to live by. Although you can avoid making up your mind, you cannot avoid making up your life. The time will come when you will demand a systematic organization of your life around a central purpose. However much you may practice holding your opinions in suspense or put off making decisions, you cannot hold your life in suspense.

Just as you know where you are going when you start off on a trip, so will you want to have a destination in mind for the journey of life. You will want to begin to build steadily in a definite sequence. Different girls may express this need for direction in different ways, just as adults do. Some will ask for a belief, others for an ideal, others for a religion. Still others may ask for a moral standard that will make the question of right and wrong clear in even the most complicated situations.

Generally, girls do not *want* anyone's ready-made opinions handed to them. They want to know how to find the answers themselves. You and other girls may begin by seesawing between doing what you want to do and what you think that you ought to do, looking to any number of standards for what that "ought" is. You may become genuinely puzzled and honestly doubtful of all set standards. You may find that the "conscience standard" does not seem to work, since other girls' consciences seem often to dictate that they do just the opposite from what your conscience tells you is the right thing. Yet these other girls, too, may be sincerely looking for help.

You do not, however, want to be one of those people who have no purpose in living. Such people stand on the side lines, amounting to little in life, because they do not know where or how to begin; they are without any goals. Although you cannot prove anything about your future, you can make up your mind about it. You must decide what attitude you will take toward it. Therefore, you must have a center, a life philosophy, around which your efforts can be unified. The quality of your life, its intent, and its direction are finally determined by your convictions, by what you want to get out of life, by what you consider most worthwhile. Around these convictions you can unify all that you do; by them you can test every action in all areas of your life. Thus you become able, in any specific case, to decide upon a particular way to act.

A self that you can depend on. Everyone has several selves. Out of these, as you grow up, you begin to visualize *the* self that you want to be. You struggle toward it, attempting to bring your behavior and your other selves in line with the better self which is your goal. Anne Frank describes your problems vividly in her diary: [1]

I have, as it were, a dual personality. One half embodies my exuberant cheerfulness, making fun of everything, my high-spiritedness, and above all, the way I take everything lightly. This includes not taking offense at a flirtation, a kiss, an embrace, a dirty joke. This side is usually lying in wait and pushes away the other, which is much better, deeper

[1] From: *ANNE FRANK: The Diary of a Young Girl*, by Anne Frank. Copyright 1952 by Otto H. Frank. Copyright 1952 by the American Jewish Committee, reprinted by permission of Doubleday and Company, Inc.

and purer. You must realize that no one knows Anne's better side and that's why most people find me so insufferable.

Certainly I'm a giddy clown for one afternoon, but then everyone's had enough of me for another month. Really, it's just the same as a love film is for deep-thinking people, simply a diversion, amusing just for once, something which is soon forgotten, not bad, but certainly not good. I loathe having to tell you this, but why shouldn't I, if I know it's true anyway? My lighter superficial side will always be too quick for the deeper side of me and that's why it will always win. You can't imagine how often I've already tried to push this Anne away, to cripple her, to hide her, because after all, she's only half of what's called Anne: but it doesn't work and I know, too, why it doesn't work.

I'm awfully scared that everyone who knows me as I always am will discover that I have another side, a finer and better side. I'm afraid they'll laugh at me, think I'm ridiculous and sentimental, not take me seriously. I'm used to not being taken seriously but it's only the "lighthearted" Anne that's used to it and can bear it; the "deeper" Anne is too frail for it. Sometimes, if I really compel the good Anne to take the stage for a quarter of an hour, she simply shrivels up as soon as she has to speak, and lets Anne number one take over, and before I realize it, she has disappeared.

Therefore, the nice Anne is never present in company, has not appeared one single time so far, but almost always predominates when we're alone. I know exactly how I'd like to be, how I am too . . . inside. But, alas, I'm only like that for myself. And perhaps that's why, no, I'm sure it's the reason why I say I've got a happy nature within and why other people think I've got a happy nature without. I am guided by the pure Anne within, but outside I'm nothing but a frolicsome little goat who's broken loose.

254

As I've already said, I never utter my real feelings about anything and that's how I've acquired the name of chaser-after-boys, flirt, know-all, reader of love stories. The cheerful Anne laughs about it, gives cheeky answers, shrugs her shoulders indifferently, behaves as if she doesn't care, but—the quiet Anne's reactions are just the opposite. If I'm to be quite honest, then I must admit that it does hurt me, that I try terribly hard to change myself, but that I'm always fighting against a more powerful enemy.

A voice sobs within me: "There you are, that's what's become of you: you're uncharitable, you look supercilious and peevish, people dislike you and all because you won't listen to the advice given you by your own better half." Oh, I would like to listen, but it doesn't work; if I'm quiet and serious, everyone thinks it's a new comedy and then I have to get out of it by turning it into a joke. I can't keep that up: if I'm watched to that extent, I start by getting snappy, then unhappy, and finally I twist my heart around again, so that the bad is on the outside and the good is on the inside and keep on trying to find a way of becoming what I would so like to be, and what I could be, if . . . there weren't any other people living in the world.

Every girl cherishes a picture of the kind of person that she wants to be, of what she wants to do in the world. The picture may not be very definite now. You may not be able to say any more about your image of yourself than that you want to be different, that you want to be above average. You have ideals for this girl whom you want to become; these ideals make her the kind of person that she is to be. Begin now to translate these ideals into reality. Your life philosophy will teach you how to reach those ideals; it will help you to decide on a way to live.

255

As you grow up, your picture of what you want to be develops. Each new experience that you have contributes in some way to your ideal. As your ethical standards, your attitudes toward people, your standards of beauty in literature, in the fine arts, and in human personality develop progressively, each clarifies the picture of what you want to be.

The things that you admire and appreciate are important in your life. Nourish the power to appreciate beauty in all its varied forms. By personal study, experience, and observation, develop your standards. Do not leave this development to chance. Remember what Martha Graham said about "cultivation of the being from which whatever there is to say comes"? In the long run, your conduct will be good according to the range and beauty of the things that you admire.

As you discover more and more of your possibilities and develop courage to attempt new and more difficult tasks, you expect more of yourself. As you come in contact with people whom you admire because they have lived radiantly and constructively, you add new dimensions to your picture of the girl *you* want to be. Unashamed, you admit the things you have not yet attained, the lack of knowledge or prejudice that held you back.

This picture of yourself as you want to be is the goal toward which you bend your efforts. The goal must be real and possible—something that you can actually achieve if you work for it. It must be developed out of your own experience, in harmony with an intelligent understanding of yourself and of your abilities. If your goal is so high as to be unattainable, it will be a cause of constant failure, a substitute for effort, or an excuse for daydreaming. If your goal is not high enough, trivial daily routines may absorb all your time, effort, and

256

Your personality develops as you participate in the give-and-take of living.

interest. For lack of challenge, you will not grow as you should.

Satisfying social relationships. One certainty about your picture of the girl you want to be is that you envision her as someone who knows she has friends and can be a friend. She does not feel alone; she is a secure, happy person because she is a part of the life about her. She has made a place for herself. How do you work toward this goal?

At first, whether you were secure or not depended chiefly on the experiences you had at home. Then came the time when you broadened your relationships. You found a new security with other groups—playmates, school groups, clubs, and church and community groups. All girls must have opportunities to experience approval and recognition outside their homes and to build ever-widening circles of friends. In this way, you develop the ability to learn from everyone; you can gain some truth from each person you know. In addition, you learn to be a friend yourself and to give affection. As you try to express your feelings for others, you develop ability to share both their happiness and their disappointments. Thus you become a more thoughtful—and more interesting—person. In this way you learn also that genuine friendship comprises give-and-take in a relationship. You find that you can hold up your end, that you have something to give, and that you can rely on yourself to make the contribution.

Little by little, you evolve a balance between self-reliance and the normal dependence we all feel. Everyone needs other people; you are dependent on your parents, on other adults, and on your friends. Are you dependent in the childish sense that you expect them to be absorbed in you or in the mature sense that we all need to take of each other's wisdom,

258

understanding, and strength? It is the give-and-take in friendship which makes a relationship genuine and meaningful.

Finding Your Place in Life

Of course, you want to be happy and successful in your relationships with many people. You want to have many different kinds of friends. Your personal friendships must be very real to you. As you grow up, however, you must begin to feel a genuine relationship to all other people in the world. Accordingly, no matter how you may arrive at what you consider worthwhile in life, no matter when you may develop a life philosophy satisfactory to yourself, sooner or later you discover that a part of a satisfactory philosophy is a hope that the kind of life which you want for yourself can be made possible for all people.

Why should this be true? Just as you discovered earlier that as a grown-up person you could not live apart from other people, so you discover now that you cannot live apart from the world. You discover that the greatest good for yourself is bound up with the happiness of other people, that the problems of the world eventually become your problems. What is right and good in your life is determined by what is right and good for society as a whole. It is in a world full of difficulties that you must work out your place. See this world as it is, with its inequalities, its hatreds, its wars; but see it also as it might be.

A self that others can depend on. Your accomplishments will be rather hollow if they cannot be viewed in terms of their value to others. One answer to the question "What is life for?" is "To teach you understanding." This world of ours is desperately in need of understanding—between

259

parents and children, between teachers and pupils, between employers and employees, among neighbors, churches, classes, races, and nations. It is not merely *important* that we learn to understand one another. It is *imperative*. Unless we learn this one lesson, we may not have the opportunity to learn others. However, you will have to work at learning understanding, and it will take a long time.

But you will want to learn understanding because you want to live. No one cares to be dead as the dodo. You will also want to report significant action when your grandchildren say, "Grandma, what did you do in those dangerous years of 1967 to 1977 when the world was poised for destruction because people might have used atomic energy against one another?"

What *can* you do? You can be aware of what is significant in your own environment. You can teach yourself understanding of what is happening today and what will happen tomorrow in your home, your school, your club, your town. You can pick up the situation you know best and make it better. You need not wait to discover what your life is for until you are called to be the first woman President of the United States!

Understanding that other people are like you. Learning understanding means developing such sensitivity to other people that, when you think of them, you are able to think of ways in which you and they are alike, not only of ways in which you differ. Wherever human beings gather together—in homes, schools, communities, or nations—we need understanding, which minimizes differences between people. Your entire future depends upon whether people throughout the world can learn to understand one another well enough so that they can live together peacefully and constructively. You may not be able to understand or do much about relations between nations. But you can do something about the human relations all about you!

It is difficult, but possible, to give up your absorption in your own interests and problems. You *can* sit down at the table and talk with your family and your friends at school and in the community about their interests and ambitions, their hopes and fears. If you talk frankly and freely, putting aside fear and distrust of people whom you once labeled "different," you will find that you are all human beings with the same basic needs. You all crave security, a sense of "belonging" and of being accepted and liked by your fellows, a feeling that you are of some use in the world. You all have fears, problems, heartaches, and limitations.

As you understand this and as you learn to put yourself into another person's place, you will find that you cannot shrug your shoulders when your little sister is unhappy and wants to tell you her troubles and that you cannot be cold and unsympathetic when your father is concerned over financial difficulties. You are unable to wash your hands of responsibility when a girl is blackballed for membership in your club because she doesn't have as much money as the rest of you or when a girl is not elected to a class office because of her race, religion, or nationality, although she obviously was your ablest candidate. You are unable to dismiss the fact that you did not speak up during discussions preceding these decisions with the remark, "It doesn't concern me." You understand how other people feel; you know what such experiences would mean to you, and you know that the girl who happens to have a different color, religion, or nationality from you

261

nevertheless has eyes, hands, organs, dimensions, senses, affections, and passions just as you have. She is hurt, as you would be, when refused an honor or a right due her.

In your home, school, and community is all the stuff of which the conflicts of the world are made—the misunderstanding, the selfishness, the prejudice, the injustice. You can close your eyes; it's easy to say, "It's not my business. Let George do it." Lots of people don't care enough about others to try to understand those who are worried and unhappy, those who haven't as much money or clothes or brains or personality, those who are pushed aside because they are of another race or religion or nationality. But the future depends upon whether you and enough boys and girls like you *are* willing to put forth the effort necessary so that people everywhere will gradually come to understand one another well enough to be able to live together peaceably instead of hating anyone or any group among them who is "different."

Only as each of us rids herself of selfishness, ignorance, and prejudice can barriers between people be removed. It is not easy to do this. You need constantly to *work* for understanding. It is not an intellectual process alone. You must do *more than talk* glibly about your concern for other people. You don't want to get into the bad habit that many adults have of talking about problems but doing nothing to alleviate them. You don't want to pronounce daringly and perform skimpily. Just raving about how bad things are, spending your energy in much talk about solutions to problems of race, prejudice, or world peace, is like frantically throwing one small pail of water on a blazing fire.

Lip service is easy, but real understanding of these problems involves action in the form of day-by-day engineering of changes in your own and other people's behavior and at-

262

titude—changes that come slowly but that *must* come before genuine solutions to these problems are found. Understanding involves eternally standing by: willing to make personal sacrifices of time, effort and money; willing to accept responsibility and take criticism and disapproval from some people; willing to lose something of yourself in other people; willing to work for changed behavior and to grow to new points of view.

In our country we do many important things in a democratic way. We do other things in undemocratic ways. Freedom and liberty do not exist *fully* for everyone. Barriers of race, color, and religion stand high even in the business world. Still higher barriers separate people from one another at the social level. Lillian Smith, a well-known writer, said: "Democracy does not make men tall; it protects men's rights to be as tall as they want to be." How tall do you want to be?

Not until everyone is seriously concerned with the welfare of others will democracy have meaning in everyday living. The problem is to learn to work and to live with your fellowmen with such sensitivity and understanding that everyone whose life you touch actually will know self-respect, dignity, and "the good life."

A country made up, as ours is, of a variety of races, religions, and national backgrounds cannot move forward if we waste our energy in antagonisms toward each other. As you work on common problems at school and in your community with boys and girls of many economic, religious, and nationality groups, you learn how to minimize racial and social antagonism. Skill in the art of living and working with other people is the dynamite your generation can use to clear its way through the granite ledge of fear and prejudice that now keeps people in our country and throughout the world from recognizing their interdependence and the common dignity of all humanity.

A concern for other people. You discover what your life is for as you contribute something of yourself to other people. As you identify yourself with larger and larger concerns and harmonize your own purposes and ideals with those of other people, you become an important link in the chain of evolving humanity.

This attitude demands faith in yourself; you cannot have faith in other people unless you have faith in yourself. The individual and society have always been bound together. What you are and what you believe will determine what you do and what you can contribute to others.

When you see yourself as a part inseparable from others, you identify your *self* with groups and individuals in such a way that your *self* is less important than your concern about what is happening to other people. This concern determines your actions day by day. Increasingly, you learn to prejudge your actions in terms of the effect they will have on the lives of others; you learn to understand cause-and-effect relationships between your past and present behavior and between your present and future behavior. You examine carefully your plans for action. You foresee and weigh consequences, think out alternatives, then revise your plans if necessary. You choose between plans on the basis of what is right for others, not only of what is right for you. You learn to act in terms of consequences you foresee—or you postpone action until the consequences can be critically and thoroughly examined.

This process assumes that you are mature enough to think and to act for yourself—and confident enough in the strength of your ideals to act in the interest of others even when such

264

action brings down on your head some unfavorable judgment. *Are* you, actually, able to guide your own conduct—or is your behavior controlled by a desire for approval, by fear of punishment, by your own selfish interest, or by your need to have someone take the responsibility for even your smallest decisions?

If you have arrived at a conviction about what is important in your life, you will not accept unthinkingly what people in authority or in your crowd demand that you either do or believe—although some things you may accept. If you accept too many things, you become an automaton, not a human being. As a mature human being, you will have developed convictions of your own—and taken upon yourself responsibility for the actions which grew out of such convictions.

Many other people, of course, will act differently from the way you choose to act. They will have accepted values different from yours as guides to their actions. Respect other people's values even though you do not accept them. Be willing to learn from someone else's experiences—but make your own judgments. Take time to form your opinions; retest and verify them as new facts appear. If not enough facts are available to make even a tentative conclusion, be willing to suspend judgment and to say, "I don't know." You do not arrive at convictions by jumping to conclusions! Moreover, it is just as poor policy to stick stubbornly to your own opinions as it is to imitate blindly the opinions of others or to accept unquestioningly prejudices, convictions, appeals to systems, and "isms" just to be different! Look for better opinions rather than for better reasons for clinging to poor opinions!

Your conviction about the importance of people becomes the touchstone for what you do with your life. Because of this conviction, you choose to do your part in the solution of problems facing the world today. These problems are so difficult and the information needed for their solution is so vast that people *must* learn to cooperate if solutions are to be found. Your skill in this area will be vital; help people, wherever you are, to talk together, to exchange ideas, to respect one another, and to work together. We must learn to take our problems in our stride, to handle them as we handle our cars and planes. Here is a cause bigger than yourself—help to create positive human relationships! Thus you will grow from egocentricity to world-mindedness. Some of you will say, "But this is religion." Many people think so. They believe that religion cannot be separated from life, that your spiritual life is just as natural as your physical life. Whether you call it religion or something else, there is something within you that generates your dreams and your ideals; you "worship and strive toward the highest you know." What you believe can never be separated from what you do. If you have a religion that is satisfying to you, it will make a difference in the way in which you live. You will stand for your beliefs. If you believe that life cannot be right for you until it is right for all people, you will not only profess that belief but you will show by your actions that you really believe it.

A willingness to work out your place in the world. One thing is certain: You are a part of this world and an heir to the society being created now. Of course, you can disregard this fact. You can sit down on the job, have no part in making the world a better place in which to live, suffer from lack of nerve, take the attitude that there is too much against you, do nothing at all. Or you can withdraw from the world, escape into daydreams, into illness, into futile blame of others or of things beyond your control.

Again, you can blithely accept things as they are, develop the attitude of being glad that the situation is no worse, glad that you are not among the poor, the hungry, the ill-housed. In this manner, you attempt to excuse yourself from doing anything to make the world better, or you pretend that you do not see any necessity for improvement.

Perhaps you may believe that the world is directed by forces beyond you, that your life is unpredictable, and that you have no control over it. You may have decided that it all depends on fate: "What will come, will." If so, be sure that this belief is not used as an excuse to cover your own laziness.

Fortunately for the world, there is another attitude. There have been people who have had the courage to say, "The world is difficult, but I was born into it. My effort can help to make it different if I am willing to look at evil but refuse to accept it. I will put my shoulder to the wheel and see what I can do about it." Out of such visions comes the inspiration to make tomorrow better than today. The world needs the buoyancy, the confidence, the eager assurance of results that a person with such courage can give.

What have you to give? First, intelligence! No matter what special abilities you may or may not have, you can be intelligent. Carlyle says that a thinking man is the worst enemy that the Prince of Darkness can have. Your first job is to think straight, to see straight. Look out at the world; see what is happening. Have an opinion about it; be able to express your opinion clearly and honestly. Say what you really believe instead of what you think that you should say.

Next, there is initiative. What world-wide benefactors are the people with daring ideas! Florence Nightingale did things that no woman had even done before; and how much poorer the world would have been without her! Edith Cavell died for her idea. Most of us are never asked to die for ideas, but all of us need to live for them. Living almost always demands more courage than dying. Jane Addams had to bear scorn, contempt, and ridicule for years because she championed the poor, the oppressed, the exploited. Could you continue your belief in your idea in spite of such obstacles?

Most important of all, yet a part of all, you can keep ever before you your deep conviction of the infinite worth of human personality. Because of that conviction, you desire the fullest possible development for each individual with whom you come in contact. You use sympathy, understanding, and love, in its broadest sense, to release personality, to encourage and stimulate its growth.

Where will you find the meaning of your life? No one can tell you that. You must pick up the situation that you know best. In all your relationships you must practice, perhaps painfully at times, the ideals that you consider big enough to strive for, big enough to live by.

It is not easy to face and try to understand difficult problems. Most people find it more comfortable just to get along with those with whom they are friendly and with the groups in which they feel safe. Only those girls who really believe that every individual is valuable and has a contribution to make will be willing to risk the new and the untried. These girls will try to work out in an intelligent fashion the difficult situations within their families, their school clubs or groups, and their communities. They will feel it their concern when a member of their family is unhappy, when a classmate is lonely or left out, when some families in their community have no decent place to live, when people anywhere in the world are hungry.

A desire to put your beliefs into action. Contributing your part to the life of the world, actually living what you believe, is a difficult task, often an unpopular one, and one that will occupy all your life. Have you ever watched a cable being swung on a huge bridge? The foundations are laid deep in several strata of rock. Then the engineers begin to spin the cable. First the shuttle carries a tiny wire across the river. Back and forth the shuttle goes, carrying a new strand each time. Thousands of times that shuttle goes over before the cable is complete. Thousands of strands of wire must be twisted into the cable before it can become a main support for the bridge.

So it is with the great ideals that are worth working for and worth living for. Some people will doubt your ideals and your convictions. There are always people to say that a thing "cannot be done." Do not let criticism or ridicule discourage you. Help to build a better world! Science has placed within our hands the means for doing it. In this past century we have seen science and architecture, even art and music, harnessed to industry to be used in its service. If enough individuals build into their life philosophies a concern for all mankind, your generation can see these mighty forces harnessed to the ideal of a better world.

Relate your life to that of the world, the part to the whole. Understand, in its world terms, the struggle for a better civilization. See your place in the struggle by whatever light you can find. Not all girls can act vigorously, but each can do something. All can stand by and see things; all can try to see things straight; and all can help others to understand

269

their significance. This is a big enough plan for anyone's life. You know already that life is futile without an ideal. Become a part of the life of the world in your own way; find a way to make your own contribution to the world. Face the future; believe and venture!

I will not say to you, "This is the way, walk in it."
For I do not know your way or where the spirit may call you;
It may be to paths I have never trod or ships on the sea
    Leading to unimagined lands afar,
    Or haply, to a star!
    Or yet again
    Through dark and perilous places racked with pain
    And full of fear
    Your road may lead you far from me or near.
    I cannot guess or guide,
    But only stand aside.
    Just this I say:
    I know for very truth there is a way
    For each to walk, a right for each to choose,
    A truth to use.
    And, though you wander far, your soul will know
    That true path when you find it. Therefore, go!
    I will fear nothing for you day or night!
    I will not grieve at all because your light
    Is called by some new name—
    Truth is the same!
    It matters nought to call it star or sun,
    All light is one.

Books You May
Want to Read

Adler, Irving, *Logic for Beginners,* The John Day Company, Inc., New York, 1964.

Bailard, Virginia, *So You Were Elected,* rev. ed., McGraw-Hill Book Company, New York, 1965.

Bauer, W. W., and Florence Bauer, *Way to Womanhood,* Doubleday & Company, Inc., Garden City, N.Y., 1965.

Choron, Jacques, *The Romance of Philosophy,* The Macmillan Company, New York, 1963.

Daly, Sheila John, *Teenagers Ask More Questions,* Dodd, Mead & Company, Inc., New York, 1964.

Duvall, Evelyn Mills, *Love and the Facts of Life,* Association Press, New York, 1963.

Duvall, Evelyn Mills, *Why Wait till Marriage?* Association Press, New York, 1965.

Duvall, Evelyn Mills, and J. D. Johnson, *The Art of Dating,* Association Press, New York, 1958.

Duvall, Evelyn Mills, and Reuben Hill, *When You Marry,* rev. ed., Association Press, New York, 1962.

Felsen, Harry D., *Letters to a Teen-Age Son,* Dodd, Mead & Company, Inc., New York, 1962.

Haebich, Kathryn, *Vocations in Biography and Fiction,* American Library Association, Chicago, 1962. Annotated book list.

Haupt, Enid, *The Seventeen Book of Etiquette and Entertaining,* David McKay Company, Inc., New York, 1963.

Haupt, Enid, *The Seventeen Book of Young Living,* David McKay Company, Inc., New York, 1957.

Johnson, Eric W., *Love and Sex in Plain Language*, J. B. Lippincott Company, Philadelphia, 1965.

Landis, J. T., and Mary Landis, *Building Your Life*, 2d ed., Prentice-Hall, Inc., Englewood Cliffs, N.J., 1964.

Mallery, David, *High School Students Speak Out*, Harper and Row, Publishers, Inc., New York, 1962.

Martin, Dolly, *Taffy's Tips to Teens*, Prentice-Hall, Inc., Englewood Cliffs, N.J., 1964.

McBain, W. N., and R. C. Johnson, *The Science of Ourselves*, Harper and Row, Publishers, Inc., New York, 1962.

Menninger, William C. (ed.), *Blueprint for Teen-Age Living*, Sterling Publishing Company, New York, 1958.

Noshpitz, Joseph, *Understanding Ourselves*, Coward-McCann, Inc., New York, 1964.

Plotz, Helen (ed.), *The Earth Is the Lord's: Poems of the Spirit*, Thomas Y. Crowell Company, New York, 1965.

Reinhold, Meyer, *Barron's Teen-Age Summer Guide*, 3d rev. ed., Barron's Educational Series, Inc., Woodbury, N.Y., 1965.

Roosevelt, Eleanor, with Helen Ferris, *Your Teens and Mine*, Doubleday & Company, Inc., Garden City, N.Y., 1961.

Ruchlis, Hy, *Clear Thinking*, Harper and Row, Publishers, Inc., New York, 1962.

Scott, Judith Unger, *The Art of Being a Girl*, MacCrae-Smith Company, Philadelphia, 1963.

Scott, Judith Unger, *The Book of Dating*, MacCrae-Smith Company, Philadelphia, 1965.

Shedd, C. W., *Letters to Karen*, Abingdon Press, Nashville, Tenn., 1965.

Splaver, Sarah, *Your Career If You're Not Going to College*, Julian Messner, Publishers, Inc., New York, 1963.

Stoutenberg, Adrien, and Laura Baker, *Explorer of the Unconscious: Sigmund Freud*, Charles Scribner's Sons, New York, 1965.

Viscardi, Henry, *A Letter to Jimmy* (A Disabled Boy), Paul S. Eriksson, Inc., New York, 1962.

White, Betty, *Teen-age Dance Etiquette*, David McKay Company, Inc., New York, 1956.

Wilkens, Emily, *A New You: The Art of Good Grooming*, G. P. Putnam's Sons, New York, 1965.

Schools and Colleges

Carter, Allen (ed.), *American Colleges and Universities*, 9th ed., American Council on Education, Washington, D.C., 1964.

Cass, James, and Max Birnbaum, *Comparative Guide to American Colleges*, Harper and Row, Publishers, Inc., New York, 1964.

Daebler, Charles, *Who Gets into College and Why*, G. P. Putnam's Sons, New York, 1965.

Eskow, Seymour, *Barron's Guide to Two-year Colleges*, Barron's Educational Series, Inc., Woodbury, N.Y., 1960.

Fine, Benjamin, *Barron's Profiles of American Colleges*, Barron's Educational Series, Inc., Woodbury, N.Y., 1964.

Fine, Benjamin, and Sidney Eisenberg, *How to Be Accepted by the College of Your Choice*, Channel Press, Great Neck, N.Y., 1960–1961.

Fine, Benjamin, and Sidney Eisenberg, *How to Get Money for College*, Doubleday & Company, Inc., Garden City, N.Y., 1964.

Gleazer, Edmund J., *American Junior Colleges*, 6th ed., American Council on Education, Washington, D.C., 1963.

Lass, Abraham, *How to Prepare for College*, David White Company, New York, 1962.

Lovejoy, Clarence, *Lovejoy's College Guide*, rev. ed., Simon and Schuster, Inc., New York, 1965.

Lovejoy, Clarence, *Lovejoy's Prep School Guide*, rev. ed., Harper and Row, Publishers, Inc., New York, 1963.

Lovejoy, Clarence, *Lovejoy's Vocational School Guide*, Simon and Schuster, Inc., New York, 1963.

Willis, Ellen, *Questions Freshmen Ask*, E.P. Dutton & Co., Inc., New York, 1962.

Index